Entrepreneur
For Teens

ANNIKA LAUNAY & BRIANA CICCHELLI

Franc World
AUSTRALIA

COPYRIGHT © 2024 BY ANNIKA LAUNAY & BRIANA CICCHELLI

All rights reserved. No part of this publication may be reproduced, distributed or transmitted in any form or by any means, without prior written permission.

Franc World Pty Ltd
Brisbane, Queensland
Australia
www.franc.world

Author's Note: The following book is a work of non-fiction. This book is a true account of the author's experiences, research and interview findings. The information provided is based on the author's knowledge and expertise in the subject matter. We encourage readers to approach the content with an open mind and to use critical thinking skills to evaluate the information presented. We hope that this book will educate, inspire and inform readers.

Book Layout © 2024 Tessa Goot

Entrepreneur For Teens / Annika Launay & Briana Cicchelli. -- 1st ed.
ISBN 978-0-6455992-7-5

Dedicated to
FRANCESCA, ANAÏS & CLÉMENCE

To our remarkable daughters,
this book is dedicated to you.

Contents

Entrepreneur

1
ACTIVATING ENTREPRENEUR MODE

Page 14

2
THE BIG IDEA

Page 26

3
SETTING UP FOR SUCCESS

Page 36

4
ALL THE PRETTY THINGS

Page 50

5
WORDS! WORDS! WORDS!

Page 66

6
SHOUT! MARKETING #101

Page 76

7
$ € £ ¥ (AKA ALL THE MONEY)

Page 88

8
STUCK FOR IDEAS?

Page 98

9
TRIALS TO TRIUMPHS

Page 110

En·tre·pren·eur

An entrepreneur is independent, self-made, confident, and capable.

She runs her own business, builds her own future, and pursues her own ambitions.

WE'RE BRIANA AND ANNIKA, SISTERS, ENTREPRENEURS AND BIG FANS OF BROAD EDUCATIONS, BRILLIANT CAREERS, AND BOLD SIDE HUSTLES. OH, AND ALSO AUTHORS OF THIS BOOK.

GROWING UP TOGETHER, WE COULDN'T STAND THE SIGHT OF EACH OTHER 82% OF THE TIME. Yet the other 18% saw us as an unbreakable team, inseparable during the heady days of the late 1980s, (yes it was a long time ago and yes, the most enviable technology was a discman – Google it).

Looking back however, that 18% of sisterly love was nearly always based around playing 'business'.

From running a hotel in the guest bedroom to creating plays, (and charging our parents for tickets), our **#GIRLBOSS** journey started long before we even knew what 'entrepreneurial' meant.

Entrepreneur

From the ill-fated lemonade stall, (we failed to consider that living on a rural property and at the end of a street meant literally not one passing car!), to our teenage formal jewellery hire business (oh the glamour!!), we loved the hustle.

Yet fast-forward to university and we chose degrees in very sensible, practical fields like journalism, science, and business, (yay, but also a bit yawn).

Luckily for us, fast-forward more time again and we've now well and truly embraced our childhood dreams. Together we've created, built and run four successful businesses including a marketing agency, a fancy cheese shop and Australia's largest platform showcasing career paths to girls – **FRANC.WORLD**.

During that time, we've learnt a thing or two about being women in business. The stories we could tell! (Though boringly, nearly all of them feature some variation of an angry little man in a cheap suit).

Anyway, what's taken us, (and others like us), years to learn, we thought to compile here into one very good-looking book so you can get a head start on building your own brilliant career.

WHAT CAREER YOU ASK? Well, that part is up to you.

You may already have your heart set on becoming a doctor, or a journalist or some other profession that has a nice, neat and ordered career path. In that case, well done! You can probably put this book down and go relax.

But what if you want to be a doctor and open your own practice, or be a journalist and start your own magazine? And what if you don't know what you want to be, but you know you want to build your own future, create your own path and be a total **#GIRLBOSS?**

Well read on, your own brilliant career might just be at hand.

Briana & Annika xx

So, what is an entrepreneur?

When people picture an entrepreneur, they often think about a person that makes millions of dollars off a crazy invention - a kitchen sponge with a smiley face perhaps, or a sunscreen you can spray over makeup.

But believe it or not, these 'crazy ideas' are actually **GREAT** solutions to problems **LOTS** of people have.

A smiley face kitchen sponge? Entrepreneur Aaron Krause was looking for a product to remove grease and oil from mechanics hands. The sponge he found worked perfectly – hard and scrubby in cold water and soft when warm. It worked so well in fact, he took it inside to do the dishes and **BOOM** Scrub Daddy was born. (PS – it makes $80 million in sales annually, that is a lot of sponges!)

> IN ITS SIMPLEST FORM, AN ENTREPRENEUR IS A PERSON WHO STARTS THEIR OWN BUSINESS...

Entrepreneur

A sunscreen you can spray over makeup? Australian Samantha Brett, had been a television news reporter out on the road in the blazing sun with heavy makeup and bright camera lights. Despite the prevalence of skin cancer in Australia, Samantha quickly found that there was no way to top up her SPF. Enter Naked Sundays SPF50+ Glow Mist Top Up Spray – the saviour of skin (and glam makeup looks) the world over!

So to become an entrepreneur, you need to identify a problem and then find a **BIG IDEA** to solve it.

Of course is not quite as simple as that, **THE BIG IDEA** may not be perfect first time round - you may need to test it and refine it, or start again entirely. Then, once you've got the perfect solution, you'll need to produce it at scale and then sell! sell! sell!

...BUT LET'S NOT GET AHEAD OF OURSELVES.

In its simplest form, an entrepreneur is a person who starts their own business based on an idea they have, or a product they create.

This could be as simple as starting your own dog-walking business, selling jewellery at the weekend markets or even babysitting.

So in short, if you have an idea or product that other people want/need and you work for yourself, **CONGRATULATIONS!** You can call yourself an **ENTREPRENEUR!**

All you need to start, is one GREAT idea.

CHAPTER 1

Activating Entrepreneur Mode

[Ask Yourself, why do you want to be an entrepreneur?]

So, this entrepreneur thing is sounding pretty exciting so far? You like the idea of working for yourself? Making your own money? Awesome. Find a comfy perch and get ready for lesson one – establishing your mindset.

Now you may be thinking, 'mindset schmindset! Let's get going already!' And we get it, (endless motivation is a great trait of successful entrepreneurs after all!) But taking the time to fully explore what it takes to work for yourself and understanding all the positives and negatives is fundamental to your journey.

So ask yourself this, why do you want to be an entrepreneur?

Is it that you have a great idea bursting out? Or that you want to make a difference in this world? Perhaps you just want to make gazillions of dollars and hang out with the Kardashians on a yacht? No judgment here!

Take some time to think about this, perhaps even put together a mood board of what want your entrepreneurial goals to look like – maybe it's being famous, or maybe it's buying 7 Ferraris or travelling the world?

Whatever your ideal future looks like, shape it now so that you know your **WHY?** Oh, and just a note on this, this is your future. You don't have to share your vision with anyone else if you don't want to, so feel free to be really honest - if it's filling the bath with raspberry jelly and diving right on in, who are we to judge?

9 Skills of a Successful Entrepreneur

WHO NEEDS A NICE TIDY LIST OF 10, WHEN YOU CAN HAVE A SHORT, SHARP LIST OF NINE ESSENTIAL SKILLS?

MOTIVATION • Let's face it, the path of self-employment is not an easy one, so staying motivated is a major skill. Whether you're in it to make a difference or gain more freedom, more authority or more money, work out your 'why' and keep focused on that.

STRATEGIC THINKING • From taking a big picture view of a situation to finding a solution no one has thought of before, thinking strategically in order to identify opportunities and achieve goals is 11/10 important.

PROBLEM SOLVING • Assess the situation, brainstorm a solution, develop a plan and execute it. Now do that multiple times a day - and usually within a teeny, tiny timeframe. GO!

ADAPTABILITY • Being adaptable, flexible, fluid, agile, (and whatever other adjectives you want to throw in here), are key to forging your own path. As Confucius said, 'be like a green twig that bends, rather than a brown one that snaps'.

FINANCIAL SMARTS • Okay this one is not that exciting, but knowing your way around a budget and profit and loss sheet is kind of a big deal - a success/failure level of importance if we're being honest. Your maths teacher does have a point when saying 'maths is crucial'. However, in saying that, we're still yet to use algebra so…

How many skills do you already have? Which ones do you need to work on? Be honest! No one is perfect at all nine — even the world's best entrepreneurs.

RISK TAKER • Enter the world of entrepreneurship at your peril! Running your own business is really just a long series of calculated risks; from backing yourself in the first place, to taking that daily leap of faith. Weigh up the pros and cons, then be prepared to jump in feet first. Every. Single. Time.

CREATIVITY • Even in the tech world, creativity is a much-needed skill. Whether it's in product development, logo design or solving a problem with creative thinking, making sure the right hemisphere of your brain is constantly switched 'on', is a must.

COMMUNICATION • Even for us introverts, (people = anxiety), being able to express and share ideas is an essential tool. Not only do you need to communicate your thoughts clearly to those around you, but to sell your business product, you need to be compelling, persuasive and even a **LITTLE** bit charismatic.

RESILIENCE • Let's face it, in the school of life, you're going to get knocked down. In the school of entrepreneurship, you're going to need to double, if not quadruple those knocks. Learn not to sweat the small stuff, be unflappable and truly believe that 'this too shall pass'.

Entrepreneur

Positives and negatives of the entrepreneur life

Positives

- The world is your oyster!
- Make your own rules
- Freedom
- Independence
- Work from anywhere in the world
- Pursue your dreams
- Set your own hours
- Do what you're passionate about
- Choose your own team
- Potential for huge financial rewards

Negatives

- A lot of hard work
- Dedication
- Long and irregular hours (especially in the beginning!)
- Initially poor pay (usually)
- Need to wear many hats (book keeper, social media guru, website specialist, packer etc)
- No guarantee of success
- Need to be financially responsible (BAS, tax, super, insurance etc)

Entrepreneur

IN YAWURU COUNTRY, (BROOME, WESTERN AUSTRALIA), THERE'S A COMMONLY UTTERED PHRASE, "TALK TO THE PEEK SISTERS, THEY'LL MAKE IT HAPPEN".
So much so, sisters Adele and Cara Peek named one of their businesses after it with Make It Happen HQ – an innovation hub and think tank providing mentorship, funding and services for First Nations entrepreneurs in the start-up and scale-up stages.

"I think our Great-Grandfather's Chinese heritage influenced our thinking, as well as our Grandmother's Indigenous heritage, which gave us a strong sense of matriarchy which has been embedded deeply in every generation of our family. We always knew where we came from and that we were part of a big, broader family. Their love and resilience really shone through us as kids, even with our pretty multicultural, sometimes rough and inaccessible education pathway."

The first of its kind in Australia, Make It Happen HQ, offers programs including a First Nation Accelerator, courses in financial literacy and ecommerce and a physical co-working hub in the heart of Broome.

Both highly respected and multi-award-winning First Nation Entrepreneurs in their own right, Adele and Cara are proud Yawuru and Bunuba women and have dedicated their lives to helping communities and businesses transform through positive change.

HOW DO YOU ENCOURAGE PEOPLE TO 'THINK' LIKE AN ENTREPRENEUR?

A big part of demystifying the process is focusing on your mindset. It doesn't matter what society labels you as, it's about having an entrepreneurial mind and spirit which influences you to be innovative and agile and creative in how you solve problems. And it's through solving problems that business ideas are formed. In simple terms it's breaking down the idea of entrepreneur so people can see its really just a process of 'how do I form an idea into reality?'

And that's what we start with when we're teaching other First Nations people. It's how do you get from point A to point B? What do you need to do and how are you going to do it? It's about identifying your goals and creating a plan of how you are going to achieve them.

A big part of it for First Peoples is also to not focus on a deficit, but instead to actually build on what we know to be true and what we already have, which is a strong First Nation base and legacy.

For our teen students, we explore this further to identify what they have personally – what resources they might have and help them unpack that because they often don't think they have anything.

As an example, most kids have a smart phone. This can help with research, ecommerce and setting up a digital platform. They may not have other privileges urban kids have, but a phone can be a great start.

We also share our stories of how we got to where we are now.

> I am a successful lawyer, a diverse entrepreneurial leader, and an innovative Cultural Intelligence Strategist. My first job was washing dishes at [restaurant chain] Sizzler.
>
> **- CARA PEEK**

> I am a subject matter expert in Aboriginal Engagement Strategies and an entrepreneur, I run multiple businesses and have a background in art curation. My first job was a checkout chick at Safeway, now known as Woolworths.
>
> **- ADELE PEEK**

Maybe one of our young girls will pick up this book and see that being an entrepreneur is possible. We want them to see that this is a pathway for them to consider, while also fully knowing that if they want to be a first nation entrepreneur it won't be the same track with the same challenges as mainstream entrepreneurs.

This isn't just about our generation. This is about bringing up the next generation of first nation entrepreneurs.

What are three pieces of advice you give to every aspiring entrepreneur?

1

ALWAYS BACK YOURSELF.

2

SURROUND YOURSELF WITH OTHER GIRLS AND WOMEN OF COLOUR FROM DIFFERENT BACKGROUNDS. Exposing yourself to different cultures and ideas is the best way to get inspiration, and while it's one thing to talk about diversity and inclusion, it really needs to be represented around your dinner table.

3

YOU ALSO REALLY NEED A PLAN FOR YOUR SUCCESS. It's very easy to have goals and aspirations, but you don't get a reputation from making things happen without having a plan in place and delivering on it.

I THINK IF YOU ASKED A FIRST NATIONS PERSON, DO YOU KNOW WHAT AN ENTREPRENEUR IS? THE MAJORITY WOULD SAY NO.

The very first barrier in that scenario is that it's a Western term. If a person doesn't even know what the word is, let alone what it looks like, how can they possibly identify as an entrepreneur? Whereas if I say to someone, for 60,000 years, our ancestors built fish traps, created bush food, survived on country and invented weapons, what do you think all of those things are? They begin to understand and identify with the term. It's about demystifying our place in society to show that actually we are descendants of the first entrepreneurs and inspiring the next generation through representation.

Secondly, we have a fundamentally different world view. We come from a community that is not predominantly a capitalist society. Western entrepreneurship is often angled at the concept of making money. Our ideas on the other hand, are usually generated out of passion or purpose, for prevention or inspiration. We tend to focus on mutual responsibility, reciprocity amongst family and we also have a cultural obligation to support community.

As a further extension of this, it's more likely that first nations people may have a lack of understanding of not only the capitalist methodology in society, but also finance and banking.

WHAT ARE SOME OF THE UNIQUE CHALLENGES FIRST NATIONS ENTREPRENEURS FACE?

Finally, the biggest problem is when you live in a remote community, you don't have the same access to services. Add in being a First Nations person and access to capital funding is also significantly reduced.

But on the flipside, the passion and purpose and creativity and resilience that actually comes from this difference in entrepreneurial mindset is what sets us apart and should be seen as an advantage. As our Mum says, if you can't get through the front door, you work out a way to get in through the window.

The Big Idea

CHAPTER 2

> **I don't have any limitations on what I think I could do or be.**
>
> **OPRAH WINFREY**
> AMERICAN HOST AND TELEVISION PRODUCER

In this section, we're simply going to work on finding a problem that exists, and then finding a **BIG** idea to create a solution to the problem.

To help you along the way, we're going to make up a scenario and use it from start to finish. Enter the first major business we launched – an online jewellery hire company. It was called 'Bijou', (French for 'jewel'), and it was very fabulous.

First Step
WHAT IS THE PROBLEM?

The first step in becoming a successful entrepreneur is to identify a problem that people have, and then come up with a good idea to fix it. So what are some problems you see around you in your community? Perhaps there are some older people that need help with garden maintenance? Or your little sister has trouble carrying her school bag, book bag and swimming stuff all at once? Or simply you have many friends and neighbours who love warm, freshly baked cookies, but they just can't be bothered baking?

Our example: Girls at high school want fabulous, standout, amazing jewellery for their school formals, but don't want to spend big dollars on items they may only wear once, (because let's face it, a diamond tiara does look a little funny when doing the groceries at Coles).

Second Step
FINDING THE PROOF

Is your idea just related to one person, or is it a problem for many people? In this step, you need to find proof to show that the problem is real and painful for your target market.

Our example: We went to four different schools and asked Grade 12 girls about their outfits and their jewellery. Some were borrowing jewellery from their mum, most were going to their local accessory store, but most either didn't find what they were looking for or couldn't afford the fabulous necklace, earrings **AND** sparkly bracelet.

Third Step
COMING UP WITH THE SOLUTION

Okay! Now we're coming to the fun part, creating the solution!

- Older people need garden maintenance? Why not set up a business offering lawn and garden care.
- Your little sister can't carry her school bag, book bag and swimming stuff? Why not design an awesome all-in-one bag that can fit everything in?
- Your friends have a lack of freshly baked cookies? Why not set up a hot cookie home delivery service that supplies baked goods every weekend?

Our example: Why not set up a formal jewellery hire company where anyone can rent fancy, sparkly jewels for their event? Our solution will be affordable, easy to use and provide the perfect finishing touch to any outfit.

Now you understand the process, get going!

Write a list of all the problems, big and small, you can see around you and how to fix them.

Good luck!

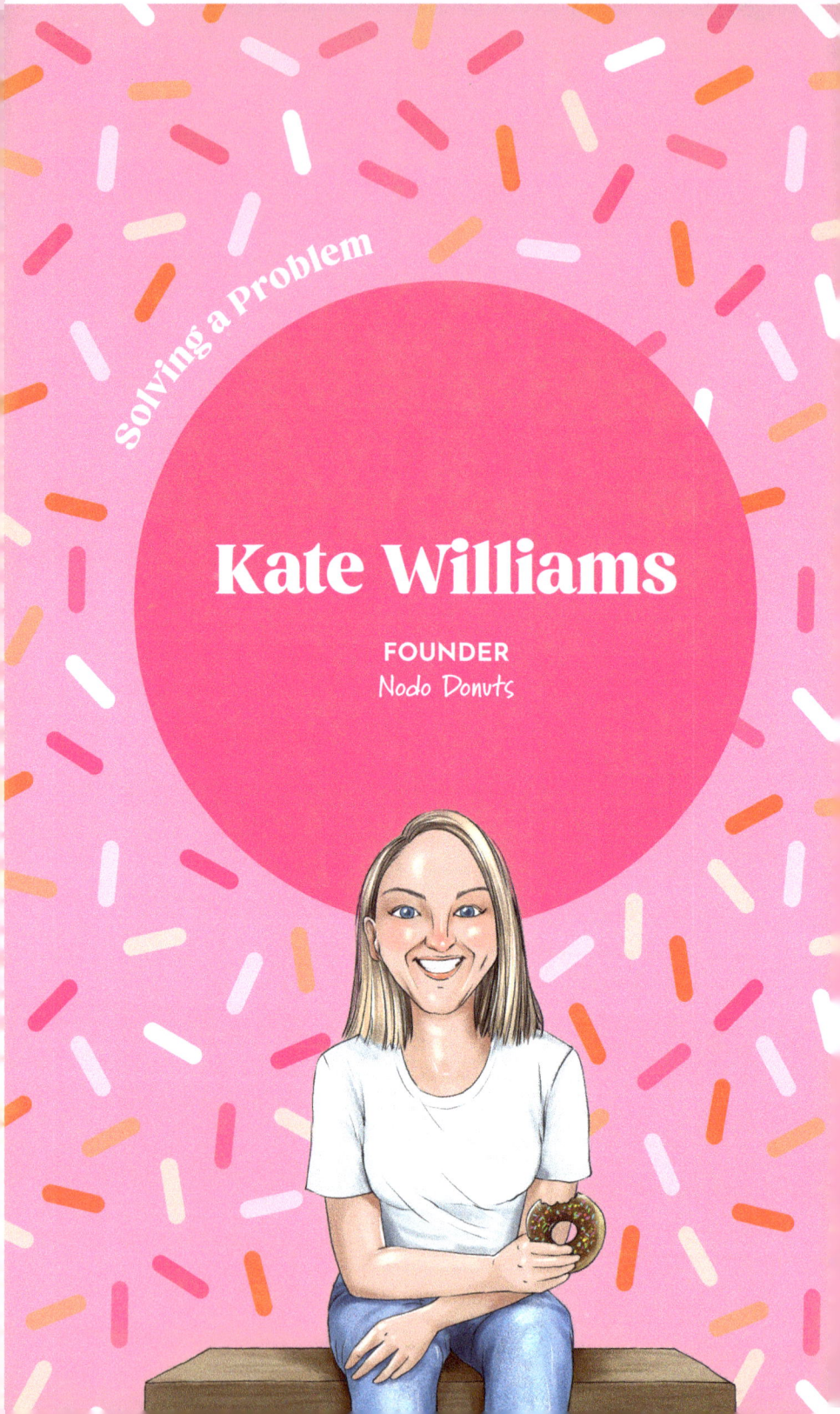

Entrepreneur

ONCE UPON A TIME THERE WAS A GIRL CALLED KATE WHO LOVED DONUTS, sadly however, her really rather serious gluten intolerance did not. So Kate set out on a quest to find a very delicious and beautifully iced donut that was also completely gluten free. Countless visits to cafes and cake shops soon followed but alas, between the stodgy, the dry and the downright gross, there were none to be found.

Undeterred, Kate decided to make her own. Six months of recipe testing, baking, (and tasting!) soon followed. From a raspberry white chocolate version to a blueberry lemon cheesecake flavour, Kate was on a mission to make the best gluten-free donut ever.

One day, as she was finishing eating a particularly luscious chocolate option, Kate realised that other people might want to enjoy her delicious goodies as well. A market stall soon followed, (which proved that yes, people did love her treats), before drum roll! she opened her very first nodo café in Brisbane.

Eight more cafes soon opened as did an additional pop-up store. A bake-at-home range was launched as well so that people all over Australia could try nodo for themselves. Before she knew it, Kate was developing yet another new flavour; birthday cake (generously topped with sprinkles no less!) to celebrate eight years of happily sharing the donut love.

Q&A

with **Kate Williams**

WHAT WERE THE EARLY DAYS LIKE FOR YOU? Starting at the markets was the most valuable experience for me. I got to speak directly with the target market and my learnings in the early days were invaluable. It really helped shape my product offering and nodo. When I finally made the decision to open the very first nodo café it was a very overwhelming experience to be honest. I don't think I was prepared for how many different hats I would have to wear. I was across all sections, baking, accounting, marketing, human resources. It took me probably a little too long to start handing over certain roles so I could focus on what I was good at. Once I surrounded myself with experts in each field, people who I trusted and were as passionate about nodo as I was, that's where the magic really started to happen.

WHAT ARE SOME OF THE KEY SKILLS YOU NEED TO START YOUR OWN BAKERY/CAFE? It sounds clichéd but you really have to love what you do and be authentic. You have to be prepared to give it everything when starting your own bakery café. Those early days when you are setting the foundations of the business take a lot of energy. If you are not authentic in your offering your staff and customers will see right through you. Your passion for what you do needs to translate down to everyone and I think that's the key.

WHAT'S BEEN YOUR BIGGEST LEARNING CURVE? It's ok not to be great at everything as a business owner. Just find people who are great, so you can focus on what you do best.

HOW IMPORTANT IS HAVING A BEAUTIFUL BRAND? Aesthetics are everything to me and I feel like everything was very considered from how our donuts and food are presented and how the products are packaged, through to the shop layout and design. My background is in marketing so I am really passionate about branding. I think it's everything in business. A brand really sets the tone and communicates so much to your audience about who you are.

WHAT DOES A TYPICAL DAY LOOK LIKE FOR YOU? When I started the business, I would be baking in the kitchen at 2am but now I am more responsible for new product development and marketing strategies to continue to build the brand.

I like to visit all the stores every week and sample the goods that we offer. Yep, eating donuts and drinking coffee is part of my job! My main focus is on making sure we have consistency across all the stores and everything is to 'nodo standard'.

Solving a problem

Kate Williams

WHEN I FIRST HAD THE IDEA FOR NODO, I DIDN'T REALLY CONSIDER THAT I WAS SOLVING A PROBLEM. FOR ME, I SIMPLY WANTED TO EAT DONUTS, BUT I COULDN'T FIND ANY GLUTEN-FREE ONES THAT TASTED LIKE THE REAL THING.

It was only when I realised there were many other people also looking for delicious gluten-free treats that I began developing recipes to produce in volume that my entrepreneurial journey really began.

By setting up a market stall I was able to test out not only my products, but the idea itself. It allowed me to prove that yes, others really were searching for a gluten-free solution, (thus proving there was a gap in the market), and yes, my products successfully filled that void.

The market stall concept also allowed for trial and error in a cost-effective way. If I didn't have that experience behind me, I would never have had the guts to open my first 'bricks and mortar' store in Brisbane.

More recently I realised people in other states around Australia wanted to enjoy our donuts. The problem was transporting them around the country and keeping them fresh, (and looking their best!). My solution was to launch a range of 'bake-at-home' gluten-free mixes that included our signature donut recipe as well as banana bread, waffles, brownies and more.

Even now with multiple stores I continue to solve problems and I always have a million plans and ideas running through my mind. I feel like we are just getting warmed up!

I am now looking to expand outside of Brisbane, knowing that we can grow without compromising the product and our current offering. I am also putting a lot of focus and energy into our blends range which I think has limitless potential.

CHAPTER

3

Setting Up For Success

Entrepreneur

If you fail to plan, you plan to fail.

NOW YOU'VE GOT YOUR BIG IDEA, IT'S TIME TO CREATE A BUSINESS PLAN.

Because as the chapter heading states, 'If you fail to plan, you plan to fail'. A business plan doesn't have to be complicated, but it's a good idea to have one in place, especially if you're planning to grow your side hustle into a larger business in the future. Your business plan should include your goals, your target market, pricing and your marketing plan.

On the next page, we've included a copy of an easy business plan called a 'lean' business plan. It only takes two pages (or one very large one!) so it's a really short, sharp way to get your idea down on paper and build out your idea.

'Lean' business plan

You don't need to complete this right now, (you're only up to chapter three after all!) but refer back to it and fill it out as you work through the book.

In the first section, write about your business idea – what makes it different, why will people buy it. The second section is where you can write down some possible names of your business, remember to keep it clear, memorable and unique. It should tell your customers what you do.

1 Business Idea
What is your big idea?

What makes your product/idea different?

2 Marketing
How will people hear about you

3 Business Name
Write down some possible business names?

Next you need to write about your target market – who are you selling to? These are your customers. Write facts about them, how old are they, where do they live. Why are they your target customer?

Next is marketing. How will you tell people about your business? If your target market all live in your suburb perhaps a letter box drop is a good

idea. Or if your market is other students, perhaps social media is a better solution for you.

Finally, pricing and profit – how much will you charge and what will your profit be? Remember your profit is how much you sell the item/service for MINUS the cost it took to create it.

'Lean' business plan
An example

So as an example, if you start up a dog walking business, you need to think of any costs associated, ($2 per dog for treats) and then the cost of the service, (say $10 per 30 mins). $10 minus $2 means you make $8 profit per half hour. If you walk three dogs together, that's $24 per half hour. If you get all three dogs to share one bag of treats your profit goes up to $28 per half hour. Great profits but sad puppies. Give them the treats for being the best boys on their walkies.

1

Business Idea
What is your big idea?

I will provide a unique dog walking service for people who love their dogs and are short on time.

What makes your product/idea different?

Dog walking, book via text so easy to do with lots of add ons like dog washing, treats, training, etc in future.

2

Marketing
How will people hear about you

Target market is local, so local Facebook group and letterbox drop while I'm walking other dogs.

3

Business Name
Write down some possible business names?

Fancy Schmancy Dog Walking

VIP DOG

A la Dogue

4. What is the problem?

Nobody in my neighbourhood has time to walk their dogs and there are A LOT of spoilt dogs.

What is the solution?

I will be a VIP dog walker.

5. Pricing

How much will your business cost to run?

Not much just leads and treats $2 per dog walk.

How much will you charge?

$10 for 30min walk

6. Profit

How much money will you make?

I can walk three dogs at once... so $30 per half hour − $2 bag of treats to share = $28 per half hour. Morning and Night sessions. $56 per day.

7. Target Market

Who are your ideal customers?

My local neighbourhood is full of people with big jobs who love their dogs and want to spoil them but don't have time to walk them and look after them.

So I'll target local community who have dogs.

Business Besties

While the idea of setting up your own business may seem like it's all fun and games and cookies, believe it or not, business can get a bit serious. As an example, you're going to have to get some official details sorted.

In Australia, this includes getting an Australian Business Number (ABN) and setting up a business bank account. If your business grows, you may also need to register for GST and get some insurance, such as public liability insurance.

While all these things sound terribly grown-up and even a little scary, fear not. Remember the big rule of entrepreneurship – **DON'T BE SCARED TO ASK FOR HELP!** Start with your parents or teachers, your local librarian and even old faithful Google.

You will probably only need the first few items on the list but remember to read through all of them to make sure your business is fully compliant with Australia's rules and regulations. If you live in a different country, the same concepts mostly still apply so read on!

Entrepreneur

- 💗 **REGISTERING YOUR BUSINESS NAME.** You must register your business name with the Australian Securities and Investments Commission (ASIC) if you are trading under a name other than your own.

- 💗 **OBTAINING AN AUSTRALIAN BUSINESS NUMBER (ABN).** An ABN is a unique identification number that all businesses in Australia must have. You can apply for an ABN online through the Australian Taxation Office (ATO) website.

- 💗 **OBTAINING THE NECESSARY LICENSES AND PERMITS.** Depending on the type of business you are starting, you may need to obtain certain licenses or permits from your local government.

- 💗 **REGISTERING FOR GST.** If your business turnover is over $75,000 per year, **(CONGRATS!)** you will need to register for Goods and Services Tax (GST). GST is a tax that is added to the price of goods and services sold in Australia.

- 💗 **KEEPING FINANCIAL RECORDS.** You must keep accurate financial records for your business. These records should include your income, expenses, and assets.

- 💗 **COMPLYING WITH TAX LAWS.** You must comply with all applicable tax laws. This includes filing tax returns and paying taxes on time.

In addition to these general requirements, there are also some specific requirements that may apply to your business depending on the industry you are in. For example, if you are starting a food business, you will need to comply with food safety regulations.

If your business is growing quickly, it may be an idea to consult with a lawyer or accountant to ensure that you are complying with all applicable laws and regulations when setting up your business.

Here are some additional resources that you may find helpful...

ASIC WEBSITE • asic.gov.au
ATO WEBSITE • ato.gov.au
BUSINESS.GOV.AU • business.gov.au

Entrepreneur

EDUCATED IN ITALY AND LIVING IN ADELAIDE, FLAVIA TATA NARDINI IS A CO-FOUNDER AND CEO OF FLEET SPACE TECHNOLOGIES, AN ADELAIDE-BASED SPACE COMPANY WHOSE MISSION IS TO CONNECT THE EARTH, THE MOON AND MARS, REVOLUTIONISING THE MINERAL EXPLORATION, DEFENCE, AND SPACE EXPLORATION SECTORS THROUGH ITS GROUNDBREAKING PRODUCTS AND CONNECTIVITY SOLUTIONS.

As a little girl growing up in Rome, Italy, Flavia Tata Nardini would relish trips to the nearby mountains to watch shooting stars turn on a light show against the night sky and dream of what might be.

"We would stay in a beautiful house in the mountains outside Roma, and for a week or two in the middle of the year you could see hundreds of shooting stars lighting up a very black sky. These were the famous Shooting Stars of San Lorenzo. I remember thinking it was the most incredible thing I have ever seen."

The shooting stars inspired Flavia to gain a Masters Degree in Space Engineering and a Bachelor Degree in Aerospace Engineering, before getting her first job – at the European Space Agency in The Netherlands.

It was upon relocating to Australia however, that her entrepreneurial spirit first took flight.

"I knew Australia was a big defence and engineering hub but when I got here, I found there was not a lot of commercial space activity and realised there was an opportunity to do something about that," says Flavia.

Her initial solution was LaunchBox, an educational company which created and launched 3D printed nanosatellites into the stratosphere with the aim of changing the way school children learn about space.

Fleet Space Technologies soon followed, launching with a history-making bang in 2018 by being the first company in Australia to send commercial nanosatellites into space.

"Our goal has always been to make satellite networks easier for people to use, not harder. We focus on low-cost solutions with improved efficiency that will help us take the next giant leap in human civilisation."

Unsurprisingly, Fleet Space has quickly grown. The company that started in a garage in Adelaide now has over 120 employees across five countries.

We're trying to simplify the industry so that space technology is not rocket science.

Some people are just born to be explorers at heart, they just want to see what's out there...

...and I can't help myself, I'm one of them.

Q&A

with Flavia Tata Nardini

WHEN DID YOU FIRST REALISE YOU HAD AN ENTREPRENEURIAL SPIRIT? I discovered my entrepreneurial spirit early on when I found joy in solving problems creatively. As a kid, I was always curious about improving things and understanding how they worked. This curiosity led me to study aerospace engineering, igniting my passion for space and technology.

Through my first startup, Launchbox, I took this mindset to a whole new level. I wanted to shake things up in how kids learn about space, going beyond the usual way of doing things. This drive for innovation has guided me through an exciting journey in entrepreneurship.

WHAT WAS THE SCARIEST PART ABOUT STARTING YOUR OWN COMPANY? Starting my own company brought a unique fear—the uncertainty. While launching Fleet Space Technologies, I held a strong vision for transforming industries through nanosatellite tech, but the market's response was unknown.

The fear of failure was real, given the responsibility to the team who believed in the vision. Their livelihoods and the company's success rested on my shoulders.

The tech landscape was complex, constantly evolving. Navigating regulations, funds, and partnerships seemed daunting.

However, this fear drove innovation, resourcefulness, and determination. I realized embracing challenges meant surrounding myself with a passionate team who embraced uncertainty. This push led to learning, adapting, and growth, teaching resilience and agility in changing times.

WHAT IS THE FIRST THING A BUDDING SPACE ENGINEER SHOULD LEARN? The first thing a budding space engineer should learn is a strong foundation in physics, mathematics, and mechanics. With these fundamentals in place, it's valuable to explore topics such as astronomy and astrophysics, coding and software, mechanical engineering, electronics, robotics, systems engineering, and space regulations.

HOW EXACTLY DO YOU LAUNCH A NANOSATELLITE? Launching a nanosatellite involves several key steps. First, we plan the mission and build the nanosatellite according to its objectives. Then, we select a suitable launch vehicle based on factors like payload size and desired orbit. After testing the nanosatellite's systems and conducting a readiness review, we launch the vehicle, deploying the nanosatellite into space.

Once in orbit, the satellite begins its operations, collecting data and performing its tasks. We actively manage its orbit to ensure optimal performance. When the mission goals are achieved or the satellite's operational life ends, the mission concludes. This process encompasses mission planning, development, launch, operations, and mission closure.

WHAT ARE YOUR THOUGHTS ON THE POSSIBILITY OF EXTRATERRESTRIAL LIFE? The possibility of extraterrestrial life is a captivating idea! The vastness of space and the discovery of potentially habitable planets hint at its potential. Our exploration of celestial bodies like Mars brings us closer to unraveling this mystery. It's a pursuit that fuels both scientific curiosity and philosophical contemplation about our place in the universe. But my 2 cents, we can't be the only ones up in this vast space.

DO YOU PLAN TO TRAVEL TO SPACE? Definitely! It's super exciting to think about humans venturing beyond our planet. With technology progressing, we're unlocking fresh opportunities that could take us to places we've only dreamed of.

CHAPTER 4

All The Pretty Things

What's In A Name?

Choosing a business name may not seem that important to begin with, but it's actually a foundational element for success. Consider it your first impression. A strong name is memorable and easy to pronounce, sticking in potential customers' minds. Imagine someone overhearing a conversation about your business - a catchy name will spark curiosity and encourage them to learn more.

A good name can also communicate your brand identity.

Frank's Fluff may sound fun, but it doesn't say much about the business – you could be selling fairy floss, fluffy toys or even belly button lint. When starting out, it's best to keep things simple and tell it like it is. Kate's Cookies, My Dog Walker and Phone Covers R US are all good examples of this.

A strong name also aids in online discoverability. If it's clear, relevant to your industry, and easy to spell, people searching for your offerings are more likely to find you. This translates to increased website traffic and potential customers.

So, invest time and effort in crafting the perfect name. It's a small detail that can have a big impact on your business's journey.

> **If you want to be original, be ready to be copied.**
>
> COCO CHANEL
> FRENCH FASHION DESIGNER & BUSINESSWOMAN

What's In A Name?

OKAY NOW THINGS ARE BEGINNING TO GET REAL - IT'S TIME TO NAME YOUR BUSINESS! THERE ARE MULTIPLE THINGS TO THINK ABOUT HERE.

YOUR TARGET AUDIENCE. Who are you trying to reach with your business? What kind of language do they use? What are their interests? Choosing a name that resonates with your target audience will help you connect with them on a deeper level.

YOUR INDUSTRY. What kind of business are you in? What are the conventions of naming businesses in your industry? You don't want to choose a name that is too out of place or that could be confused with a competitor.

YOUR BRAND IDENTITY. What do you want your business to be known for? What kind of image do you want to project? Your business name should be consistent with your brand identity and help you achieve your marketing goals.

THE LEGALITIES. Make sure your business name is available as a trademark and that it is not too similar to the names of other businesses in your area. Google 'check trademark Australia' and a bunch of free options come up.

THE MEMORABILITY. Your business name should be easy to remember and pronounce. If people can't remember your name, they're less likely to do business with you.

THE WEB-FRIENDLINESS. Your business name should be easy to type into a web browser. If your name is difficult to spell or pronounce, people may be less likely to find your website.

THE LONGEVITY. Choose a business name that you won't outgrow. If you plan to expand your business in the future, you don't want to be limited by your name.

Some tips to get you started...

BRAINSTORM A LIST OF WORDS OR PHRASES that you think of when you think of your business. This could include your products or services, your target audience, your brand identity, or your company culture.

USE A THESAURUS OR ONLINE WORD FINDER to help you come up with new words or phrases.

ASK FRIENDS OR FAMILY for their suggestions.

Once you have a few names that you like, **TEST THEM OUT WITH POTENTIAL CUSTOMERS OR CLIENTS**. Get their feedback on which names they like the best and why.

DON'T BE AFRAID TO CHANGE YOUR NAME if you're not happy with it. It's better to choose a name that you love than to be stuck with one that you don't.

Once that's done, you will probably need to create a logo. This will be more important for some businesses than others.

Mood Board

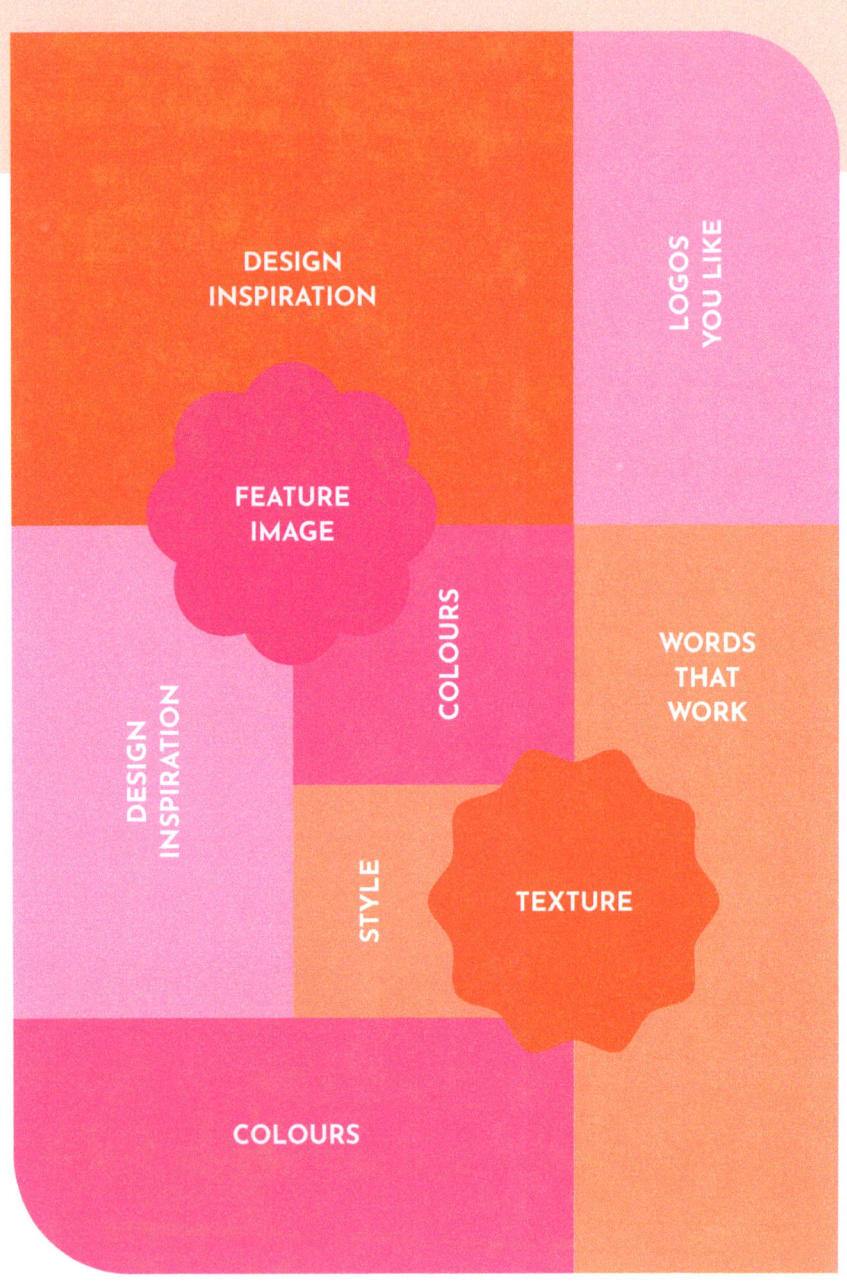

Branding

IT IS NOW OFFICIALLY TIME TO MAKE YOUR BUSINESS LOOK PRETTY! This is big **YAYS** all-round as we create Pinterest boards, spin colour wheels and get our graphic design on.

First up, you need to get some inspiration. To do this, we need to create yet another trusty mood board. Start by putting your business name in the centre, (don't worry, we'll work on that in a minute!) Then, fill the page with colours, logos, pictures and brands that inspire you and make you think '**YES! THIS IS EXACTLY WHAT I WANT MY BUSINESS TO LOOK LIKE!**'

As per your lean business plan, consider your target market and your business. What is going to make you stand out?

Next you need to pick out the colours your brand is going to be. This might be one or two or even three. Add them to the mood board, and if you need some help, have a look at the section on colour psychology.

Logo!

A LOGO IS A GRAPHIC MARK, EMBLEM, OR SYMBOL THAT IDENTIFIES A COMPANY OR ORGANIZATION.

Logos are often used in marketing materials, such as websites, business cards, and product packaging. They can also be used on social media and in advertising.

A good logo should be simple, memorable, and relevant to the company or organization it represents. It should also be scalable, so that it can be used in a variety of sizes and applications.

To create your own logo there are a lot of 'free' logo makers online (once again – Google!) otherwise Canva is a great tool for this with a massive library of online templates to work with.

IF YOU'RE UNFAMILIAR WITH THE SUPER AWESOME DESIGN TOOL THAT IS CANVA, THEN PREPARE TO BE AMAZED.

Within minutes you'll have everything from business cards to flyers designed with this easy-to-use and very user-friendly platform.

Once you're in your design platform, you'll need to work out what to create. The basics are:

Business Card

- Your business name
- Your contact information
- Your logo
- What you do (AKA your tagline)
- Your social media handles

Social Media Tiles

A social media tile is a small, square image that is used to promote your business or brand on social media. While photos of your dog and what you ate for lunch are cool, these ones are more business in that they usually contain your logo and a message for your audience such as sale on now or buy my book etc.

Social media tiles are a great way to increase brand awareness and

Flyer

All details as per the business card, then:

YOUR OFFER • What are you offering? This could be a discount, a free trial, or a special event.

YOUR CALL TO ACTION • What do you want people to do? This could be to visit your website, call your phone number, or sign up for your email list.

VISUALS • Visuals are a great way to capture people's attention and make your flyer more memorable. You can use images, infographics, or even videos.

TIP!

Social media tiles come in a variety of sizes, so make sure you choose the right size for the platform you're using. For example, Instagram tiles are typically 1080x1080 pixels, while X (formerly Twitter) tiles are typically 1600x900 pixels.

drive traffic to your website or social media profiles.

You may need other items like posters, web banners and other branding materials, but these are the basics to get you started!

Bonus Section

Psychology Of Colour

THE PSYCHOLOGY OF COLOUR EXAMINES HOW DIFFERENT COLOURS INFLUENCE OUR EMOTIONS, BEHAVIOURS, AND PERCEPTIONS.

Each colour has its own unique psychological impact, and understanding these effects can help us in making brand choices and designing marketing strategies.

Red, for example, is a colour often associated with intense feelings. It can evoke strong emotions and increase our heart rate, making it an excellent choice for capturing attention or creating a sense of urgency. That's why you often see red used in clearance sales or advertisements.

On the other hand, blue is often associated with feelings of calmness, serenity, and stability. It has a soothing effect on our psyche and can promote relaxation and concentration. Many organisations and companies that aim to convey trustworthiness, dependability, and professionalism choose blue as their primary colour. Banks and law firms, for instance, often incorporate blue into their logos and branding.

Have a closer look at the below colour wheel to find out what colour encourages optimism and creativity, which palette exudes luxury and which tone is associated with health and well-being!

Remember, everyone may interpret colours differently and cultural influences can also affect their meanings.

Colour Wheel

- **Red**: Action, Love, Adventure, Energy, Strength
- **Pink**: Femininity, Respect, Creativity, Intuition, Calm
- **Purple**: Spirituality, Fantasy, Imagination, Justice, Royalty
- **Blue**: Success, Trust, Security, Confidence, Power
- **Green**: Safety, Harmony, Health, Nature, Loyalty
- **Yellow**: Clarity, Positivity, Warmth, Fun, Curiosity
- **Orange**: Emotion, Freedom, Optimism, Original, Enthusiasm

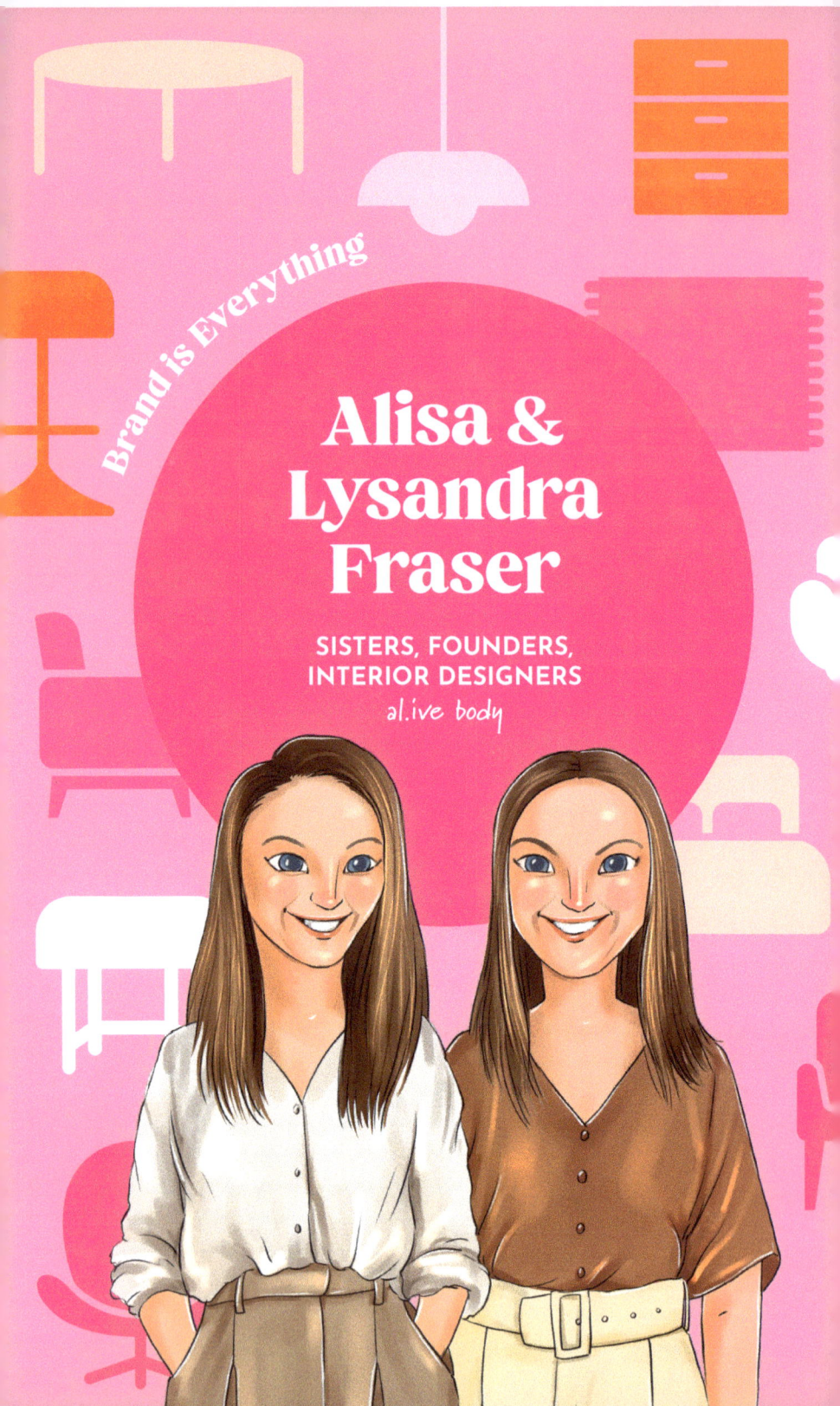

Entrepreneur

IDENTICAL TWIN SISTERS ALISA AND LYSANDRA FRASER WERE BOTH BUILDING CAREERS IN THE POLICE FORCE WHEN THEY DECIDED TO APPLY TO TAKE PART IN POPULAR HOME RENOVATION TELEVISION SERIES THE BLOCK: SKY HIGH.

Not only were they successful in their application, but they went on to win the series with their beautifully curated interiors and elevated design skills.

They also proved so popular with viewers that they were asked back to do a second series, (The Block: Fans vs Favourites), which then saw them hand in their police badges and dive into the world of interiors and entrepreneurship full time.

Since then, the sisters have founded Alisa & Lysandra interiors, worked on residential and commercial projects, delivered multiple brand collaborations, created their own brand al.ive body, which offers beautiful products for the home, bathroom and body, and filmed a renovation series The Design Duo.

(Did we mention that they also live next door to each other in beautiful homes they built together?) – awesome!

Entrepreneur

WHAT ADVICE DO YOU HAVE FOR YOUNG PEOPLE WHO ARE PASSIONATE ABOUT INTERIOR DESIGN BUT DON'T KNOW WHERE TO START?

We always say start with your friends and family. Ask them if they want you to make over a room, because until you get your hands dirty and actually experience the work and skills that it takes, you don't really know whether it's for you. Interior design is so instinctual, you really need to have a natural talent so starting out like this, or even on your own room is vital.

Next, look at homewares shops, magazines and design sites for inspiration, then put together a mood board.

Have a play around with the layout of your furniture, get some posters or some artwork from Etsy and frames from IKEA. Go to the shops and look at their displays then just start playing. Get some terracotta pots and paint them, bring greenery in then start layering your bedding. Curate a look you love and learn from there.

Once you think interior design is for you, undertake qualifications. Then it's all about work experience - ask firms whether you can come in and spend a week with them and learn as much as you can.

With any job, when you start out you make silly mistakes but then over time, you study and absorb and improve and eventually, you can look back at how far you've grown and developed as a designer.

Entrepreneur

If you want to do something and you want to do it badly enough, anything is achievable – we are living proof of that.

We weren't great at school. We didn't have the easiest upbringing, but we know hard work and dedication. As long as you've got that and you've got drive, you can be anything you want to be.

Brand
Every

It might start out initially being about colours and logos, but it quickly morphs into so much more. It represents your business and what you stand for and is the reason why your business will or will not be around in 20 years' time.

It's also about the emotion that somebody feels when they experience your business or look and touch your products and services.

In our line of work a lot of the emotion comes from products being visually pleasing, which is again why our brand strategy is so important.

With our product range al.ive body, we wanted to create something that was functional and environmentally responsible, but above all, aesthetically pleasing.

We took a huge amount of time in choosing the colours, especially

is thing

for the packaging, to ensure each product went with as wide a range of interiors and design styles as possible.

Across the range we've utilised soft pinks, sage greens, neutral sand tones and even a charcoal – all derived from natural elements and all absolutely beautiful. When we see them now in magazine spreads, on television and in other people's homes we're always so proud of how they look.

The aesthetic vibe also extends through to our logo, website and social media – every touch point of our brand.

We want to get to the point where people see our logo and instantly purchase, because they know anything from al.ive body will be of high quality, environmentally conscious and a beautiful addition to their lifestyle.

CHAPTER 5

Words! Words! Words!

Okay now, this chapter is going to be a bit tricky where we throw around some pretty advanced marketing terms.

Tagline

Elevator Pitch

Motto

Slogan

Unique Value Proposition (UVP)

Key Messages

Unique Selling Proposition (USP)

ARE YOU FAMILIAR WITH ANY OF THESE?

While they're all a little bit different, they essentially do the same thing – they either tell your audience/clients/buyers about you, about what you do, why they should care about you or ultimately; why they should buy from you **AND** they all do it in as few words as possible.

LET'S LOOK AT SOME FAMOUS SLOGAN EXAMPLES:

> Melts in Your Mouth, Not in Your Hands.

M&M

> Expect More. Pay Less.

TARGET

> Maybe she's born with it. Maybe it's Maybelline.

MAYBELLINE

> A Diamond Is Forever.

DE BEERS

Now it's your turn.

THINK ABOUT YOUR BUSINESS.

What do you do?

Why are you unique?

What problem are you solving?

Believe it or not, writing as few a words as possible is actually **REALLY** hard. To make it a bit easier, write a sentence to each of the questions above. Don't worry about making them short, just focus on writing the best answer you can.

We're going to use an example of a delicious cookie company, (mainly because we're hungry and the thought of hot, fresh chunky cookies filled with melty choc chips is giving us serious goals right now.)

What do you do?
We sell homemade cookies and post them direct to your door.

Why are you unique?
We are the only company in our area to do 24 hour delivery.

What problem are you solving?
The freshest, tastiest, chunkiest cookies straight to you.

Now let's highlight the **KEY** messages.

> **What do you do?**
> We sell homemade cookies and post them direct to your door.

> **Why are you unique?**
> We are the only company in Tasmania to do 24-hour delivery.

> **What problem are you solving?**
> The freshest, tastiest, chunkiest cookies straight to you.

Now let's try and work those bits into one sentence.

> The freshest, tastiest homemade cookies in Tasmania, delivered to you in 24 hours.

Finally, let's see if we can make it any snappier/quirkier/funnier.

> Tasmania's chunkiest cookies;
> 24 hour delivery

BOOM! Job done. Wasn't that hard now, was it?

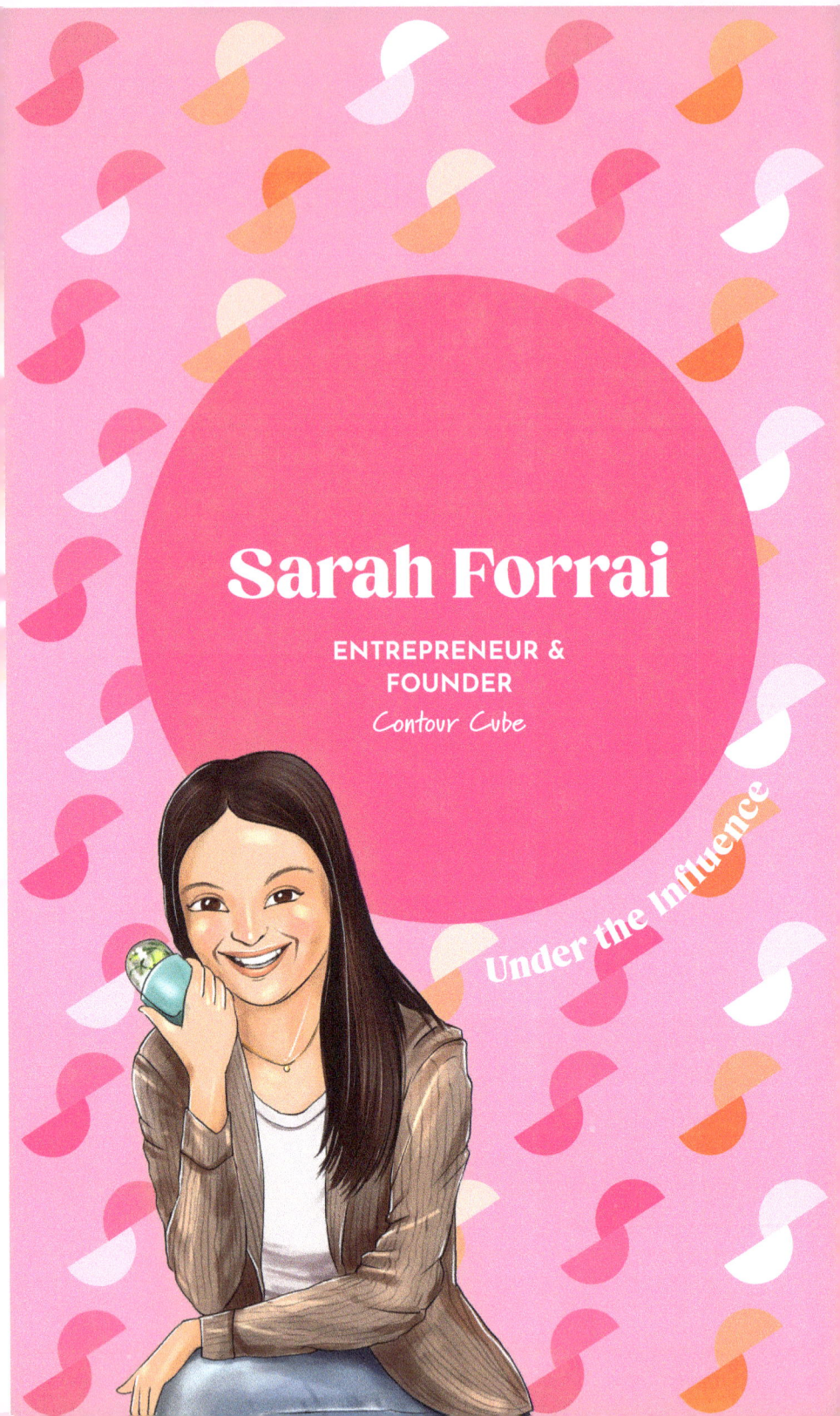

Entrepreneur

AS WITH MOST BRILLIANT BUSINESSES, SARAH FORRAI FOUNDED CONTOUR CUBE BY CREATING A SOLUTION TO A PROBLEM. She loved her morning ice facial, (rolling ice over the skin to tighten and brighten), but hated how awkward, messy and slippery the whole process was.

"My mum first got me onto icing my skin each morning. It's great as an instant wake-me-up that is used by celebrity facialists, makeup artists and aestheticians, but there was no tool to make the whole process easier. That really surprised me – that there was a gap in the beauty market. We had a 3D printer at home so I tried designing something myself that would easily grip the ice as well as fit the contours of your face.

Within a couple of hours we had a 3D printed prototype in our hands, which was just crazy. It then took a couple of months, but once we were happy with the shape and logo, we finalised our beautiful colour palette, added some final touches like our heart shaped filling hole and hit go on production of our first batch of contour cubes!"

The Influence of Influencers

At the same time we were launching Contour Cube, I'd stumbled upon the 'small business' side of TikTok. I was so drawn to the authenticity and relatability of the content - the behind-the-scenes of business, like packing orders. I was keen to launch our product on TikTok and use the platform to test the market. It just resonated with so many people so quickly, not just within Australia, but around the world. So I guess from that moment, it really encouraged us to lean into social media even more. It was a great way to build an online community, but also get real time feedback from our customers as well, which was really helpful in launching new products after that.

THEN, CAME A VIRAL POST, AND THE POWER OF CELEBRITY.

Quite early on one of our posts went viral. We sold out very quickly and had to think about mass production. We expanded our colour range with help from our online community and even got feedback from customers wanting a smaller travel size - which we delivered. We also started posting every day to understand our customers better. Retailers also wanted to start stocking our products which was so exciting.

Then one day we woke up and wondered why we had so many sales overnight. I checked my phone and had all these messages from friends – (supermodel and influencer) Kendall Jenner had posted about us. My mind was blown. It was an organic post from her and it just transformed our business.

We then appeared on (business reality television series) Shark Tank, and successfully gained the support of four investors.

Appearing on Shark Tank and getting four investors was a huge deal for our business. It was like a big thumbs up from very successful industry leaders who believed in what we were doing and wanted to be a part of it.

Not only did they invest money but they provided mentorship as well. I think having mentors who have been through the challenges of scaling a business and the ups and downs of the business journey is a game changer. It was also wonderful that they saw the potential in our business and wanted to help us accelerate our business growth to new heights with their support.

Can you give us three tips for growing a business with social media?

1

BE CONSISTENT. Keep showing up consistently and making content daily if you can. From there, I think you'll understand what your audience wants to see from you and you'll be able to align your content with your audience's interests.

2

The other thing would be to **BE AUTHENTIC** and tell your story, be honest and transparent and share your experiences in a personal way. Also make sure you're not afraid of showing your personality and adding humour in your videos.

3

LASTLY, CREATE CONTENT THAT INSPIRES, EDUCATES AND ENTERTAINS. Those are the three categories I normally think of before I start creating content and I think that will help you make really engaging videos or posts for your audience.

In the rollercoaster ride of business...

...those highs come and go so celebrate every little win and keep pushing forward.

CHAPTER

6

SHOUT!
Marketing
#101

Entrepreneur

Once you have everything in place, you need to start telling people about your business, this is called...

MARKETING AT ITS CORE IS THE PROCESS OF CONNECTING YOUR BUSINESS WITH YOUR TARGET MARKET.

Whether you tell people about your business, hand out flyers, give out samples or place an advertisement, these are all ways of connecting you to your buyer.

The best way of considering what marketing channel is right for you is to consider your target market, (your buyers). Who are they, what do they read/watch/listen to, where do they go? Now find a strategy that is suited to them.

Here are some examples:

Letter Box Drop

You want to be a window washer? Print off some flyers and place them in letter boxes of every house that has lots of windows, (or even better, really dirty ones!)

Flyers

Want to be a photographer? Print some flyers of your work (maybe even colour postcards) and distribute them to local shops and venues. If you want to be a family photographer, try your local play centre. If you want to photograph food, try local cafes and restaurants.

Word Of Mouth, Referrals

Want to be a tutor? You need to reach the parents. Tell every parent you know and if you have one or two students, tell them they get a $5 discount for every friend they refer to you.

FREE

Entrepreneur

Online Listings

Want to host children's birthday parties? Reach a wider audience by posting online to local Facebook groups about your services – adding a photo of you dressed in your best costume will also help attract attention.

FREE

Get Involved In Your Community

If you are a dog walker, you could volunteer at your local animal shelter or join a dog walking group. This would give you the opportunity to meet potential clients and learn more about the needs of dog owners in your area.

FREE

Offer A Free Trial

Want to decorate shop windows? Why not offer to do a prominent local business for free? In exchange leave some business cards with them to hand out to other local businesses in the area.

Competition

If you want to sell jewellery, why not try running a competition on social media? Giveaways are a great way to get new followers (and new buyers!) – just make sure to follow guidelines for online competitions! These can be found online.

Partner With Other Businesses

If you have set up a mobile spray tanning business, partner with someone who does make-up or hairstyling. You can cross promote to each other's clients and even put together offers which promote both businesses together.

Advertising

Paid advertising can be very expensive, the best way to do this cost effectively is in local community newspapers and magazines. If you want to do lawn mowing and landscaping why not try advertising at your local sporting club – lots of parents will be there busy watching sport instead of keeping their lawn tidy!

A Story In The Newspaper

Ring up or email your local news team and see if they'd like to do a story on you and your business. Remember all press needs to know three things:

1. THE HOOK • What is different, special or unique about your business – Are you the youngest ever? Are your cookies doubling in sales every two weeks? Do you walk 14 dogs at a time? (We don't recommend this one!)

2. THE DETAILS • Who are you, what are you doing, when are you doing it, where are you doing it, how are you doing it.

3. THE PLUG • Make sure you mention your business' name and contact details so people can get in touch!

FREE

Don't sit down and wait for opportunities to come. Get up and make them.

MADAM C J WALKER • AMERICAN ENTREPRENEUR AND PHILANTHROPIST

Entrepreneur

IT ALL STARTED WITH A CAMEL CALLED PATRICK. NAUGHTY, NAUGHTY PATRICK.

Growing up, I always wanted to be an actress. I went to film school and was balancing my work on the farm with playing roles in movies and commercials but the more time I spent on the farm, the more I wanted to merge the two together. Starting a TikTok account was really just my way of merging my performing and my love of education and entertaining with camels and farming.

When I first started out, I really just wanted a way of making people laugh. And I thought that maybe I could make a few videos go viral to help the business out but mainly I was doing it for me. I wanted to show people what my life was like and get to do something creative while farming.

So I started making videos about super cool camel facts. Like camels have belly buttons and can survive 15 days without water. I was building traction with that.

#cameltok

My mum, who started QCamel, is a huge inspiration to me, but she doesn't really understand how social media works. She asked me if I could just create a viral video. I explained that its not really how it works, you can't just 'create' a viral video. But then one day I filmed this really random thing about a baby camel called Patrick who had escaped. I didn't think about it too much, I didn't really edit it. I just filmed and uploaded and that was it. The next morning it had over a million views, I couldn't believe it, it had gone viral. I was like, 'See Mum? You asked and I delivered!'

My TikTok account really blew up from there. I've since gained over 14 million likes on my videos, been nominated for a TikTok award and now trend on the term #cameltok!

From a business perspective it's been really powerful as well. We've seen a 20 to 30 percent increase in product sales and a 50 percent increase in tourism. We're now looking into crowd funding to launch the next stage of QCamel.

Advice for young people looking to utilise social media for their business?

 # NUMBER ONE IS THAT IT'S REALLY IMPORTANT TO BE YOURSELF and that's easier said than done. I'm a giant dork, okay? I film with no makeup on, covered in poo and dirt and hay and sweat. I'm often a bit sunburned, (which is not good - please wear sunscreen!) There's not a lot of gloss about what I do, so I am true to who I am in every way possible. I really connect with people. I think people forget that social media is social. It is not about selling yourself or a product, it's about connecting with people. So that's the biggest thing that I would say, is really figure out who you are and be happy with that.

ALSO, DON'T OVER THINK IT. When I was first starting out and wanting to grow my following, I'd think about when America was waking up and when Australia was going to bed and try to post at popular times. I'd look at hashtags and tap into TikTok trends and I'd make conscious decisions about things, but overall, you can't get obsessed with it. You cannot sit there and obsess over views and numbers and comments. It will drive you nuts.

 # THE FINAL THING IS TO LEARN RESILIENCE. Really, really learn resilience. I delete comments, I block people. If there are trolling comments I call them out and use it as an opportunity to educate people or make something positive out of it. But I think it's also important to know that it's okay to close the comments or to turn your phone off and just walk away. I'm over 30 and I can see the good and bad side of social media and recognise that it's only one small part of life or business.

What does a typical day look like for you?

Well as with most entrepreneurs, it's like five people's jobs in one. There is no one typical day. This morning for example, I'm being interviewed, then I have to go and film some content down on the farm – it's a promo that I've got to do for Binge, the streaming service. Then I've got an audition to do for a major Australian Bank's promotional campaign which is awesome. Then I'll probably be doing a little more farm work and then a bit more marketing work. Yesterday, I was processing and bottling all the milk.

Earlier in the week I was down at the farm herding camels and feeding them. So I do lots and lots and lots of different things. **THERE'S NO TYPICAL DAY!**

You have to believe in yourself, take risks, and ignore the doubters.

NAOMI SIMSON • ENTREPRENEUR & FOUNDER

CHAPTER

7

$€£¥
(AKA All The Money)

For most entrepreneurs money is not the driving factor. Let's face it, an entrepreneur often has to put their own money in to start a business, (this is called bootstrapping just FYI), and then there is no promise of regular pay. However, like eating your greens and tidying your room, it is something you have to deal with.

Firstly, when setting up a business there are nearly always costs. You may need to buy items like raw ingredients, tools or products to get started, then you may need to pay to print flyers or build a website. Finally, there may also be fees just to start your business.

Before you actually decide to move forward with your idea it's important to do your research and put together a spreadsheet so you know what it is going to cost you to get started.

Then of course you need to think about how much you're going to charge for the product/service you're offering. Again, look around and do your research, what do other similar businesses charge? If you're offering a skill that has a creative side such as art, design or creative writing, remember to always place a true value on those skills – because if you don't, no one else will!

Finally, don't forget that big scary thing called tax. In Australia currently, you can earn $18,200 before having to pay any tax. This is called the tax-free threshold.

Now don't get us wrong, this is a **LOT** of money for any tween or teen to make in their business, ($350 a week!) but just keep an eye on your numbers – if you even get close to this figure (and **CONGRATS** by the way!) you may need to call in your mum, dad, teacher, grandma or your friendly local bookkeeper/accountant for advice.

The Basics of Profit and Loss

Understanding basic profit and loss is crucial for running a successful business because it helps you track how much money you're making or losing. This knowledge can guide business decisions, show financial health and keep your entrepreneurial dreams alive!

Calculating profit and loss may seem overwhelming, but it's really just basic math - simple addition and subtraction.

FOLLOW THESE STEPS

Add up your **TOTAL INCOME** (money earned)

Add up your **EXPENSES** (money spent)

Find the **DIFFERENCE** by subtracting total expenses from total income

The outcome is your **PROFIT** (a positive number) or **LOSS** (a negative number)

Here's a real world example. You are selling ice blocks at school during summer (yes please!). You purchase a pack of 20 ice blocks for $5.50. You then price each one at $1.00 to sell to your friends. The exercise is a raging success and you sell every one!

TOTAL INCOME	20 x $1.00 = $20.00
TOTAL EXPENSES	$5.50
DIFFERENCE	$20.00 - $5.50 = $14.50
PROFIT/LOSS	$14.50 profit!

Believe in your business and trust the numbers!

To be driven by passion is more likely to bring success than to be driven by money.

It's an unrealistic notion that money makes you happy.

CAROLYN CRESWELL • FOUNDER
CARMAN'S FINE FOODS

Entrepreneur

GROWING UP IN ENGLAND, NAOMI WAS SUPER STUDIOUS AND LOVED PARTICIPATING IN ALL THINGS EXTRA-CURRICULAR, FROM DANCE CLASSES AND ORCHESTRAS, TO SINGING IN CHOIRS. She also participated in as many school excursions as possible, which were often to London to see live shows and stage productions, lucky thing!

On moving to Australia she built a career as a singer and leading Australian theatre performer, reaching the semi-finals of The Voice (Season 4), being part of the Australian cast of Beautiful: The Carole King Musical and performing alongside renowned artists including Ricky Martin, Tim Finn, Guy Sebastian and Kate Miller-Heidke.

Spreading her entrepreneurial wings, she has since gone on to co-create The Little Red Company – a music-led theatre production company which produces dazzlingly fabulous productions which to date, have played to over 3.2 million people.

...others will only value what you value...

Think about any business or any industry or service, you don't ride the bus for free, you don't get chocolate for free, you don't get McDonald's for free, people don't live rent-free. You pay for everything in life, but it seems that there is a dynamic that has been set up whereby artists are expected to give what they do as a job for nothing.

I'm not talking about singing at your Grandma's birthday, but more for events and concerts where the reasoning is 'but it's for charity!' or 'it will be great exposure!'

Singers particularly, seem to get asked to sing for free a lot, but on the flipside, orchestras don't. When there's 60 people on stage, you don't expect that 60 people are going to show up and play a Beethoven concerto for nothing. But people will often expect that because you're just one person and it's your voice and it's part of your body, that singing is just something you can do. They don't see the hours that you spend training and they don't see that your health impacts your ability every single day - how much sleep you've had, how much water you've drunk, it all counts. We have to be just as disciplined as athletes and sports stars when it comes to our bodies being able to do what we've trained them to do, but that's not reflected in the money on offer.

I always think if you're a performer, it should be a very, very rare moment that you give somebody a performance for nothing and it should be because you believe in what you're supporting or you're gifting it to somebody that you love. And then other than that, always ask for something in exchange.

My advice to young artists is always ask people for something, whether it's $20 or $100, and also always tell them what you would have charged if you weren't discounting your rate.

If someone comes to me and says, 'I'd like you to sing - it's for a great cause' - and I want to get involved - I always tell them, 'no worries, absolutely, I'd love to come and support, but just so you know, if I was charging you, this is how much my fee would be.' Because I think that maintaining your value is really important.

This discussion in arts has become particularly critical in the last few years with crises around the world; drought, bushfires and with all sorts of environmental issues or sickness. Artists are the first people that are called upon to donate their services, but then when the COVID -19 pandemic hit, artists were the first people to lose their job and the last people to get back on the tools.

I think something I've learned over the last 20 years has been that others will only value what you value. If you don't value yourself, your time and your skills, you can't expect other people to value it. I think when it comes to putting a price on creativity, if you're willing to give away what you do for a living, for free, then people will become less inclined to pay for it in the future.

Entrepreneur

A word on business – diversity

Being an entrepreneur in the arts industry, the biggest thing I've learned is to diversify, to have a diverse set of skills and not just be good at one thing.

There are some people like elite concert violinists; that is their one thing, and they will just do that for the rest of their life and be the best in the world at it. But those people are like 0.0001% of the population. For the rest of us who want a career in this industry, you have to be good at a lot of different things. And it's the same with running a business. My business doesn't just produce theatre, we also create events for clients. We also have an education program. We also run a community choir. We have so many different things that we offer that are all part of the same creative ethos and artistic vision, so we have lots of different ways that people can intersect and connect with our company that aren't just reliant on buying a ticket.

THIS IS ONE OF THE KEYS TO OUR SUCCESS.

Stamina · **Determination** · **Grit**

What do you need to succeed?

CHAPTER 8

Stuck For Ideas?

> **NOW HAVING GOTTEN THIS FAR THROUGH SUCH A SUPER EXCELLENT BOOK, WE'D ASSUME THAT YOU HAVE A PRETTY GREAT IDEA YOU WANT TO LAUNCH OUT INTO THE WORLD. BUT IF YOU DON'T, THAT'S OKAY!**

There are endless possibilities when it comes to starting a business. Do some research online and in your community to see what businesses are already out there and what gaps there might be. You can also talk to friends and family.

If you still can't think of where to start, here are ten super cool ideas to get you thinking…

Baking

Do you enjoy baking and decorating cakes and cookies? If so, consider selling your baked goods to friends, family, and neighbours.

Window Washing

Most homeowners don't clean their windows as often as they should, and all you need to get started is a glass cleaner and a high-quality squeegee/window scrubber. Start by asking homeowners in your street.

Jewellery Making

If you're interested in selling jewellery, create different styles that will appeal to people of all ages, including kids, teens, and adults. These could be sold to friends, at the local markets or even on Etsy.

Gift Wrapping

Buying a gift for someone is one thing, but wrapping it is another. Learn different wrapping techniques to make each wrapped gift eye-catching and unique. This could be even be done in partnership with your local shopping centre around Christmas.

Holiday Decorating

Some businesses and/or homeowners in your neighbourhood may want to put up holiday decorations, but don't have the time. Offer to decorate for them. There are plenty of stores that offer cheap décor (especially after the event has passed) and renting out your items can make even more income.

Website Design

Computer savvy? Create a well-designed website for a local business owner who doesn't have one. To make even more money, offer to maintain it.

Photography

Many families—especially those with young children—love having their photos taken for keepsake purposes. Get started on a photography business by taking photos of a family you know.

Landscaping

You know your neighbourhood best: is there someone, perhaps an elderly neighbour, who would appreciate you mowing the grass, planting a garden, and/or tending to the flowers on their property?

Social Media Marketing

If you enjoy Instagram, TikTok and any other social channels, and can take a good photo, put your skills to good use and help local business owners smarten up their accounts.

Tutoring

If you excel at a certain school subject, set an hourly rate and provide tutoring services to your fellow classmates and/or young children.

BONUS IDEA

Love kids and are full of energy? Naturally good at the dramatic arts? Why not put your services forward as a kids party entertainer? You could host fairy parties, be a face painter, a balloon artist or even dress up as a favourite character like Elsa from Frozen or Buzz from Toy Story.

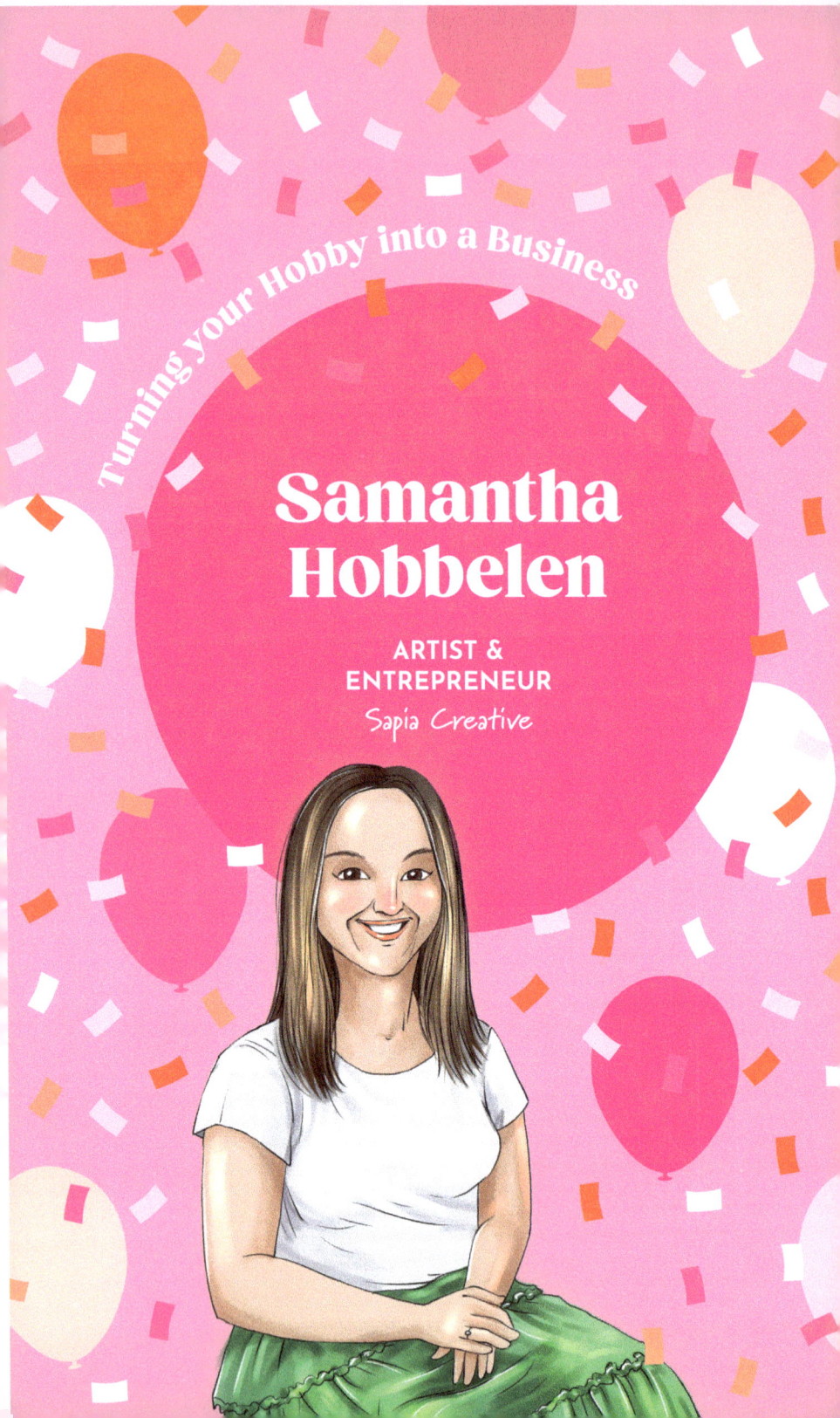

Entrepreneur

I STARTED ART AS A CREATIVE OUTLET ONLY. IT WAS NEVER MEANT TO BE A BUSINESS. It was never meant to have a commercial aspect to it. But as my confidence grew, as my creative practice grew, I was able to look at it as a business opportunity and ask myself, 'Can my art fill a gap in the market?' 'Am I filling a need?'

I then became more strategic and began to look at similar emerging artists and go, okay, so what are they charging? What have they done?

Having started, run and sold several other businesses in the past, I was able to look objectively at my art and ultimately decided that yes, I could turn my hobby into a business.

12 Tips to Consider
WHEN TURNING A HOBBY INTO BUSINESS

01 NUMBER ONE IS TO CREATE AND KEEP CREATING because as you hone your skill, you will start to find things will flow, things that you thought were hard to create before, will become easier. Your skill will intensify.

02 AS A CREATIVE ARTIST YOU NEED TO HAVE OTHER SKILLS, you need to be very organised, highly motivated and you need to be able to step back and be very discerning about what might work in a market and what's not. It's not enough just to be creative, you need to have business skills as well.

03 BE BRAVE AND PUT YOUR WORK OUT THERE. Just share it. There's something very vulnerable about creating something from nothing and putting it into a marketplace. It takes huge confidence, but just do it.

04 AND MORE ON CONFIDENCE, HAVE CONFIDENCE IN YOUR PRICING. If you know you have a great product or service, you will find your market at a fair price. This can sometimes take time to learn, but once there. Stick to your guns.

05 HAVE PERSEVERANCE, GRIT AND TENACITY. The experience that you will get from each micro lesson and each thing from your first month in business and then your first six months really does create a snowball effect.

06 BE CLEAR TO YOUR VISION AND NOT BE SWAYED BY WHAT OTHER PEOPLE THINK. Everybody is going to have an opinion about what you do, what you don't do, how you do it, how you don't do it. You need to stand firm.

07 SOCIAL MEDIA HAS SOME NEGATIVES, BUT IT CAN ALSO BE USED FOR GREAT GOOD. Use it to your advantage and show off your work on any or all platforms. You may just find your community!

08 LOOK TO ONLINE SALES PORTALS. Beyond Etsy, there are incredible platforms you can reach out to like Blue Thumb in Australia that are very open and actually champion emerging artists.

09 DON'T BE AFRAID TO SHOW OFF YOUR WORK IN PERSON. If you have an opportunity to sell at your local markets, do it. The skills that I learned doing markets are grassroots lessons that you can't learn unless you're face-to-face with a potential buyer.

10 HAVE YOUR ELEVATOR PITCH PERFECT, because people want to know what you do in 10 seconds.

11 ALWAYS BE LEARNING, everything changes all the time and so you need to constantly be open to feedback and taking on new things.

12 GET A MENTOR. If you can get someone who is willing to give you their time and expertise, take it. Usually they'll be at least three steps further along in their creative journey and with their advice, it should allow you to get from A to B that bit quicker.

Entrepreneur

What's your first memory of being an entrepreneur?

My parents used to own a motel in Toowoomba where I grew up. I remember I was forever thinking about ways of selling things. I would laminate gum leaves and sell them as bookmarks in the reception. I started a little babysitting service when I got to a certain age at the motel. I just thought that everyone was wired that way; that you wanted to do something creative and help people, but also get some pocket money from it.

> I am still in progress, and I hope that I always will be.

MICHELLE OBAMA • LAWYER, AUTHOR & FORMER FIRST LADY OF THE UNITED STATES

Famous Australian Female Entrepreneurs

Here are some amazing Australian female entrepreneurs that are killing it in their fields!

MELANIE PERKINS
Co-founder and CEO of Canva

JANE LU
Founder and CEO of Showpo

JANINE ALLIS
Founder of Boost Juice Bars and investor on Shark Tank Australia

KYM ELLERY
Fashion designer and founder of ELLERY

PIP EDWARDS
Co-founder and Creative Director of activewear brand P.E Nation

MARYANNE SHEARER
Founder of boutique hotel chain The Art Series Hotels

LORNA JANE CLARKSON
Founder of activewear brand Lorna Jane

CAROLYN CRESWELL
Founder of Carman's, a successful muesli and health snack brand

NAOMI SIMSON
Author, entrepreneur, and Shark Tank Australia investor

KIM HERAS
Co-founder of accelerator program Startmate

Entrepreneur

JULIA GILLARD
Former Prime Minister of Australia and chair of the Global Partnership for Education

KAYLA ITSINES
Fitness entrepreneur and co-founder of Sweat

MICHELLE BRIDGES
Fitness trainer, author, and TV personality

KRISTEN BOSCHMA
Co-founder of Thankyou, a social enterprise that sells consumer products to fund development projects in third world countries

EMMA ISAACS
Founder and Global CEO of Business Chicks

CYAN TA'EED
Co-founder of Envato, a global marketplace for digital assets

JULIE STEVANJA
Co-founder and CEO of Stylerunner, an online activewear retailer

ELLE MACPHERSON
Supermodel and founder of WelleCo, a health and wellness brand

SAMANTHA WILLS
Jewellery designer and founder of her eponymous brand

ALARNA LONG
Founder of fashion brand ELK Accessories

TARYN WILLIAMS
Founder and CEO of The Right Fit, an online talent platform for the creative industry

ERIN DEERING
Co-founder of Skoolbag, a communication platform for schools

KATE MORRIS
Founder and CEO of Adore Beauty, Australia's first online beauty store

JO BURSTON
Founder and CEO of Inspiring Rare Birds, a global community for female entrepreneurs

JESSICA RUDD
Co-founder of luxury baby product brand Jessica's Suitcase

9 Trials To Triumphs

Success is not final, failure is not fatal: It is the courage to continue that counts.

JANINE ALLIS
FOUNDER - BOOST JUICE BARS

Learning From An Epic Fail

Whether we like it or not, and no matter how bad it feels at the time, failure is a necessary step on the road to success.

Every entrepreneur experiences failure at some point in their career. What's important is firstly, to have a good cry while eating an **ENTIRE** pack of TimTams. Then, turn your epic fail into a valuable lesson.

Learning From An Epic Fail

HERE ARE SOME OF THE THINGS THAT ENTREPRENEURS CAN LEARN FROM FAILURE...

WHAT WENT WRONG?

The first step to learning from failure is to identify what went wrong. This can be a difficult and painful process, but it is essential to understanding the mistakes that were made. Once you know what went wrong you can start to develop strategies to avoid making the same mistakes in the future.

WHAT DID I LEARN?

In addition to identifying what went wrong, it is also important to reflect on what you learned from the experience. This could include learning about the market, the competition, or your own weaknesses, hint: no one is perfect!

HOW CAN I IMPROVE?

Once you have identified what went wrong and what you learnt, you can start to develop strategies to improve your chances of success in future. This could involve changing your product or service, your marketing strategy, or your business model.

IF YOU'VE GONE THROUGH AN EPIC FAIL AND FEELING A BIT DOWN ABOUT IT ALL, TAKE HEART, EVEN SOME OF THE WORLD'S MOST SUCCESSFUL ENTREPRENEURS CAME BACK FROM INITIAL FAILURE.

WALT DISNEY was fired from his job at a newspaper because his boss told him he lacked imagination and had no good ideas. However, Walt didn't give up on his dreams. He went on to create some of the most iconic and beloved characters in the world, including Mickey Mouse and Donald Duck.

MICHAEL JORDAN was cut from his high school basketball team. However, he didn't let this failure stop him from pursuing his dream of playing professional basketball. He went on to become one of the greatest basketball players of all time.

STEVE JOBS was fired from Apple, the company he co-founded. However, he didn't let this failure deter him from his entrepreneurial ambitions. He went on to found NeXT and Pixar, two other successful companies before eventually returning to Apple and driving it to momentous success.

Building Resilience

RESILIENCE IS THE ABILITY TO WITHSTAND OR RECOVER QUICKLY FROM DIFFICULTIES. As the entrepreneurial journey is so full of challenges, the ability to bounce back from setbacks is critical.

Here are a few tips for building resilience as an entrepreneur:

EMBRACE FAILURE. Failure is a part of the entrepreneurial process. Every entrepreneur will experience failure at some point. The important thing is to learn from your failures and use them to grow and improve.

HAVE A POSITIVE ATTITUDE. A positive attitude can go a long way when you're facing challenges. It can help you to stay motivated and focused, and it can help you to see opportunities in the midst of adversity.

BE ADAPTABLE. The business world is constantly changing, so it's important to be adaptable. Be willing to change your plans when necessary, and be open to new ideas.

HAVE A STRONG SUPPORT SYSTEM. Having a strong support system of friends, family, and mentors can be invaluable when you're facing challenges. These people can provide you with encouragement, advice, and help when you need it.

TAKE CARE OF YOURSELF. It's important to take care of your physical and mental health, especially when you're under stress. Make sure to get enough sleep, eat healthy foods, and exercise regularly.

TAKE BREAKS. When you're feeling overwhelmed, it's important to take a break. Step away from your work and do something you enjoy. This will help you to clear your head and come back to your work refreshed.

CELEBRATE YOUR SUCCESSES. It's important to take the time to celebrate your successes, no matter how small they may seem. This will help you to stay motivated and on track.

DON'T GIVE UP. There will be times when you want to give up. But if you keep going, you will eventually achieve your goals.

> The more you praise and celebrate your life, the more there is in life to celebrate.

OPRAH WINFREY
AMERICAN TALK SHOW HOST, PRODUCER, AUTHOR

Entrepreneur

BIG, BEAUTIFUL, FABULOUS EYELASHES HAVE BEEN THE BASIS OF ANGELA KENNEDY'S BUSINESS FOR OVER FIFTEEN YEARS. From applying lash extensions to a few clients in the front room of her home, Angela has built Lash Envy into an empire, with five salons throughout Melbourne (Victoria), a training academy and an online lash supply store.

I never liked school, but I have always loved to work. One day I came home from school and announced to my mum that I had gotten a job at the local supermarket. Mum looked at me like, 'what?'

After school I joined a skincare business in a sales role. By 26 I was the most successful performer in the Asia Pacific region, but by the time I reached 30 I was burnt out. I took four months off for the first time in my life to re-evaluate and reset.

Fast forward a few years and I'd moved to Ireland where I decided to train as a lash extension artist. I told myself to just keep things small, I wanted a simple job that I could fit in around having a family, but I guess once an entrepreneur always an entrepreneur and Lash Envy was born!

Resilience

Resilience goes hand-in-hand with starting a business.

You're going to have little hurdles right from day one. Sometimes you'll get a horrible client that no matter what you do, you will never please. They'll go straight to Google and write horrible things about you, yet never tell you to your face, so you never have the opportunity to repair things. Things that can damage your reputation really beat up your soul when you're in this sort of business.

Mostly I try to not take things personally. I realise that if somebody is attacking me verbally or on Google, it's not really about me. Most people are just projecting whatever is going on in their world, so I always try to look at it through that lens, that it is not really about me, it's their cry for help.

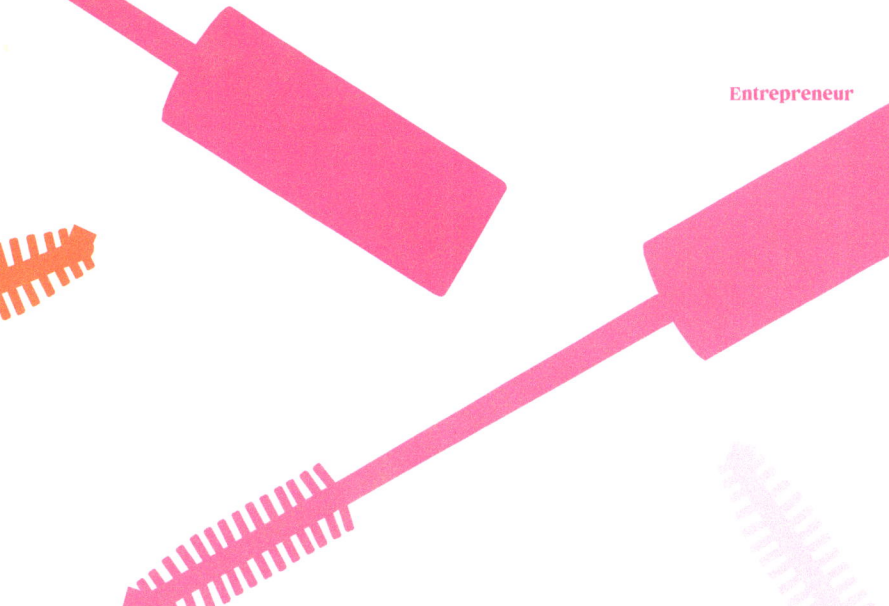

In saying that, if someone is unhappy with you or your business, it still hurts.

So I'm always trying to work at becoming more resilient. One thing I do to support that, is exercise. I think that's really important because it clears my mind. I don't exercise for my physical health so much. I don't exercise to lose weight. I exercise for my mental health to keep me feeling disciplined, strong and able to cope. It gives me energy so that I'm not tired because when you're tired, you can't cope with things effectively.

Also don't make quick decisions. I never make a decision when I'm feeling bad, because it's not a proper decision. I'm not making it on logic. I'm making it on feelings, so I try to constantly make a decision when I feel good. Continuing on from this, I would never quit when I felt bad. I would consider quitting when you're feeling good about everything because that's when you know it's for the right reason.

Finally, never make decisions late at night and always try to compartmentalise your problems. So say, okay, I'm not going to think about it today, but at five o'clock tonight I'm going to allow myself an hour to think about it, then I will make a decision. If no answer comes to me then, I tend to sleep on it because the universe always seems to give you the answer you need – when the time is right!

Entrepreneur

A word on business – finance

I see a lot of women who start beauty businesses but fail very quickly because they might be awesome at hair or they're awesome at makeup or they're awesome at lashes, but they have absolutely no understanding of how to run a business and they end up running themselves into the ground.

MY BIGGEST ADVICE HERE IS DON'T SPEND MONEY THAT YOU HAVEN'T MADE. Don't start with a fit out of a $200,000 shop for example, that's just foolish. Start small and work your way up slowly and spend the money that you have made and build from there. Don't just go all in at the beginning, otherwise you're starting from a drowning point.

Being successful in business requires you to experience some inevitable failures and setbacks.

Your resilience and ability to adapt, learn, grow and spring back quickly will be what sets you apart.

The Social Entrepreneur

Final Word

Imagine you have a friend named Sarah. Sarah loves animals and cares deeply about the environment. One day, she notices a problem: there are too many stray dogs and cats in her neighborhood. They don't have enough food, shelter, or medical care. Sarah could have just felt sad about this, but instead, she decides to do something about it. That's where being a social entrepreneur comes in.

Being a social entrepreneur means using your passion and creativity to make a positive change in the

Being a social entrepreneur means using your passion and creativity to make a positive change in the world

world. It's like being a superhero, but instead of fighting villains, you're fighting social and environmental problems.

Social entrepreneurs are like regular entrepreneurs, the people who start businesses, but they have a special focus. They don't just want to make money; they want to make the world a better place. They come up with innovative ideas to solve social issues, just like how Sarah wants to help the stray animals.

Social entrepreneurs can work on all sorts of problems. Some might focus on providing clean water to places that don't have it, while others might work on improving education for children in need.

The key is that they are driven by a desire to create positive change and help others.

What's amazing about social entrepreneurship is that anyone, including teenagers like you, can become a social entrepreneur. It doesn't matter how old you are; if you have an idea and the determination to make it happen, you can be a social entrepreneur.

So, if you see a problem in your community or the world that you care deeply about, don't just feel sad or frustrated. Think like a social entrepreneur. Use your passion and creativity to come up with solutions, and who knows, you might just change the world for the better!

Entrepreneur

GROWING UP IN RURAL NEW SOUTH WALES, A TWO-HOUR BUS TRIP TO SCHOOL AND BACK WAS THE NORM FOR HANNAH VASICEK. While the ride was long and sometimes boring, it gave Hannah her very first experience at being an entrepreneur – although she didn't quite realise it at the time.

Sitting on the bus everyday, I soon realised that kids would be pretty hungry on the ride home, so I started buying a box of candy strips for $20. I'd buy a hundred candy strips and I'd sell them for a dollar each. Instant profit. Soon I was selling two boxes a week, that's $160 profit a week at 13! Then mum took me to a beading shop, I made my first pair of earrings and I loved it, so I started selling jewellery to friends and teachers in the staff room.

When I turned 16 we moved to Tasmania. At this stage I was making so much jewellery that I started a market stall - but I still saw myself as someone who had a hobby, not a business. It wasn't until I had started Uni, probably five years in, did I begin to think of myself as an entrepreneur.

Entrepreneur

For me, 'entrepreneur' wasn't a term that I had heard a lot of growing up, which I think is really sad. I'm very passionate about it being a known career for young people. I think intuitively I was an entrepreneurial person growing up because I was really excited about marketing and sales and making something. But I didn't realise I was an entrepreneur until well into my journey.

That journey has now seen Hannah (and her sister Rachel), launch and grow Francesca, an award-winning jewellery brand that now has flagship stores in Hobart (Tasmania) and Melbourne (Victoria) and legions of loyal fans around the world.

Beyond beautiful jewels, the brand has a strong focus on giving back, and to date has donated over $1million to Australian charities.

I always say to aspiring entrepreneurs that outside of making money, a successful entrepreneur needs to know their values – what is it that brings joy, what makes you fulfilled? Everyone is different, but for me, my values are empowering people and having a purpose.

A few years into our journey, as we started to become more successful, we wanted to build something that gave our team purpose outside of just selling jewellery. That's where the giving back component of Francesca came from - a deep personal need to have a purpose of bringing awareness to causes that we were really passionate about.

So we began to sell products that weren't just jewellery, but had meaning.

Giving Back

Initially, we started working with the Breast Cancer Foundation, and then a local charity called Be Hers, which raises funds to rescue women and children from human trafficking.

We now create 12 bracelets throughout the year where we raise funds and awareness for different charities and have just hit over a million dollars in donations, which is incredible.

We have two models for raising funds. The first one is where 100% of the purchase price goes to the charity. We wear the production cost and all other costs involved so that our customer can buy a piece of jewellery and know that every dollar they spend is going to a good cause.

We did this for the bushfire appeal bracelet, where we made a conscious decision for 100% of the purchase price to go to the appeal. We literally raised $100,000 in two days and had to stop sales because there was no way we were going to fulfill any more orders!

Our other model is our sustainable charity model where a percentage of profits goes to the charity. You might buy an awareness bracelet for $59 and then $20 of that purchase goes to the charity. That means we still have money to market the bracelet, we have money to pay our team who make them down in Tasmania, we have money to purchase more product – the charity model is sustainable. Not every business has a lump of cash they can donate to charity month on month, but in this way we can continue the concept year-round with 12 different charities and give so much money because we are able to cover our costs.

What are three keys to your success?

1 **Passion**
You need to love what you do!

2 **Conviction**
You need to believe in yourself.

3 **Perseverance**
You need to be consistent and keep at it!

> My favourite thing about being an entrepreneur is the excitement of always having something to learn. There's always something to improve on. And I love the freedom that being an entrepreneur gives you.

Entrepreneurial Terms

BUSINESS PLAN • A detailed document outlining goals, strategies, and financial projections for a business venture.

CROWDFUNDING • Raising capital from a large group of individuals, typically through online platforms, for business projects.

E-COMMERCE • Buying and selling goods or services online through websites or digital platforms.

ENTREPRENEURIAL MINDSET • A way of thinking that focuses on creativity, problem-solving, and seizing opportunities for growth.

ENTREPRENEURSHIP • The process of starting and running a business, taking on financial risks in the pursuit of success.

FRANCHISE • A business model where individuals purchase the rights to operate a branch of a larger company's established brand.

INNOVATION • Introducing new ideas, methods, or products to improve existing systems and drive growth.

MARKETING • Promoting and selling products or services through strategic campaigns to attract customers.

MENTOR • An experienced individual who provides guidance, support, and advice to help entrepreneurs succeed.

NETWORKING • Building relationships and connections with other professionals to exchange ideas and opportunities.

OUTSOURCING • Hiring external contractors or services to handle specific tasks or functions within a business.

PITCH • A brief presentation to investors or potential partners outlining the business idea and its potential benefits.

PROFIT • The financial gain earned by a business after deducting its expenses from its revenue.

REVENUE • The total income generated by a business from its sales or services.

RISK-TAKING • Willingness to take calculated chances or risks in business decisions to achieve long-term success.

SCALING • Increasing the size and scope of a business to reach new markets and expand operations.

SOCIAL MEDIA • Online platforms and websites used for networking, marketing, and promoting businesses to a wide audience.

START-UP • A newly established business typically characterized by innovation, creativity, and rapid growth potential.

SUSTAINABILITY • Operating a business in an environmentally and socially responsible manner for long-term success.

VENTURE CAPITAL • Funding provided by investors to start-ups and small businesses.

Acknowledgements

In the acknowledgements section of a book, the authors usually list all the very important and helpful people it takes to put a book together, from the editors, agents and research partners through to various dogs for keeping laps warm and husbands for making endless cups of tea.

However Annika and I have wanted to write a book for a very, very long time. So long in fact, we wanted to start our acknowledgements with our school teachers who first encouraged us to write, (**MS LANSKEY, MRS BRUGMAN, MRS WISE** – we're looking at you!) But of course, that was going to make our list even longer than the book itself.

So, constraining ourselves to some, (but by no means all!) of our favourite people in a short succinct manner, here goes;

Thank you to the brilliant **TESSA GOOT** for your incredible work in designing the book – your fun and flair has really bought it to life!

To **JENNIFER SHARP** for your guidance and editing support.

To every single one of our **AMAZING INTERVIEWEES**, for your generosity in sharing your knowledge and wisdom with our readers – Thank you!

REBECCA DURRANT, MARGARET MILTON AND THE ENTIRE TEAM AT QBD BOOKS – your unwavering support of our vision has been simply incredible and we are so grateful to have you with us on this journey.

To **MUM AND DAD**, thanks for having us! If it wasn't for you, we wouldn't have our super awesome sisterly bond. Thank you also for instilling in us both a love of learning, writing, travelling, eating, history and that big old entrepreneurship bug that keeps driving us to bigger, better, shinier and newer things.

Finally to **ALL THE GIRLS**, (including our daughters **FRANCESCA, ANAÏS** and **CLÉMENCE**). Thank you for inspiring us to write this book. Thank you for all your dreams of bright futures and fabulous jobs and financial independence and career satisfaction, we wrote this for you.

> **Being a woman in business doesn't come without challenges.**
>
> **My advice? Surround yourself with other supportive women that encourage you, share ideas, and get you motivated.**

JESSICA ALBA • AMERICAN ACTRESS & FOUNDER · THE HONEST COMPANY

About Franc.World

At **FRANC.WORLD** our mission is to introduce the world of careers to every Australian tween and teen (9-18 years).

WHY? BECAUSE IF YOU CAN SEE IT, YOU CAN BE IT.

By showcasing career paths and educational opportunities, we can empower every Australian youth, (and especially girls), to reach their full potential, regardless of gender, race or postcode.

WWW.FRANC.WORLD

About The Authors

BRIANA CICCHELLI

ANNIKA LAUNAY

BRIANA CICCHELLI and **ANNIKA LAUNAY** are sisters, writers, entrepreneurs and BIG fans of broad educations, brilliant careers and bold side hustles.

BRIANA is a qualified journalist and also has an Arts major in archaeology, (just in case she ever stumbles across an undiscovered ancient burial site). **ANNIKA** meanwhile, has several fancy letters after her name due to an honours degree in Business Management and a degree in Science with a major in psychology.

Together they run a national marketing agency, have opened a restaurant and fromagerie (that's a fancy way of saying cheese shop), run **LOTS** of race horses and have created Franc.World - Australia's largest multimedia platform dedicated to showcasing career paths for tweens and teens.

About Francesca

Meet **FRANC** – Franc (or Francesca) is our namesake, muse, chief inspiration and our **WHY** for creating **FRANC.WORLD**. She is bold, vivacious and a natural extrovert who loves food, fashion, travel, horse riding and the beach - but doesn't really love maths or chores.

One day, she'd like to become a fabulous fashion designer or an actor or maybe an influencer or a shoe/jewellery designer or an interior designer or a fashion stylist to the stars. She has no plans on becoming an accountant.

Coming Soon

STEM
For Teens

The Ultimate Guide to your future career **STEM FOR TEENS** – How to be a veterinarian, engineer, archaeologist, chemist, astronomer and more…

Fashion
For Teens

The Ultimate Guide to your future career **FASHION FOR TEENS** – How to be a jewellery designer, celebrity stylist, brand buyer, couturier, trend forecaster and more…

Notes

Notes

Notes

Notes